DATE DUE

DEMCO 38-296

History of the
Modern World

Volume 1

Origins of the
Modern World

Marshall Cavendish
New York • London • Toronto • Sydney

Marshall Cavendish Corporation
99 White Plains Road
Tarrytown, NY 10591-9001

ty

isconsin–Milwaukee

Editor: Timothy Cooke   *Associate Editors: Robert Anderson, David Scott-Macnab, Casey Horton*
Design: Wilson Design Associates   *Picture Research: Jenny Speller, Adrian Bentley*
Maps: Bill Lebihan   *Index Editor: Kay Ollerenshaw*

Library of Congress Cataloging-in-Publication Data

History of the modern world / [editor, Timothy Cooke].
    p. cm.
    Contents: v. 1. Origins of the modern world—v. 2. Religion and change in Europe—v. 3. Old and new worlds—v. 4. The Age of the Enlightenment—v. 5. Revolution and change—v. 6. The changing balance of power—v. 7. World War I and its consequences—v. 8. World War II and the Cold War—v. 9. The world today—v. 10. Index
    Includes bibliographical references and index.
    ISBN 0-7614-7147-2 (set).—ISBN 0-7614-7148-0 (v. 1).—ISBN 0-7614-7149-9 (v. 2).—ISBN 0-7614-7150-2 (v. 3).—ISBN 0-7614-7151-0 (v. 4).—ISBN 0-7614-7152-9 (v. 5).—ISBN 0-7614-7153-7 (v. 6).—ISBN 0-7614-7154-5 (v. 7).—ISBN 0-7614-7155-3 (v. 8).—ISBN 0-7614-7156-1 (v. 9). ISBN 0-7614-7157-X (v. 10).
    1. World history Juvenile literature. I. Cooke, Timothy, 1961- .
D20.h544 1999   99-14780
909.08—dc21   CIP

Printed and bound in Italy   07 06 05 04 03 02 01 00 7 6 5 4 3 2 1

Publisher's Note

In 1997 Marshall Cavendish Corporation published the twelve-volume *History of the Ancient and Medieval World* to critical acclaim and the appreciation of school teachers newly challenged by the need to expand their teaching of world history. Our ten-volume *History of the Modern World* picks up world history where our previous set left off. Beginning with an overview of the political, social, and religious elements that engendered the modern world, the first volume also examines the technological and intellectual transformations associated with modernism. Volume one then establishes a basis for understanding the internal histories of Africa and Asia. Subsequent volumes examine in greater detail the cultures, politics, and leaders of nations and empires throughout the world.

   The writers and editors of this encyclopedia have aimed to present the story of the modern world in simple but dramatic terms, portraying both the wide currents as well as the critical details of world history. Individual chapters focus on special themes and particular regions to press the world story forward in a framework that encourages continuous reading and also permits reference usage of specific sections. Particular attention has been paid to inclusion of cross-references to related themes and regions of the world.

   Visual resources were selected for the historical information they convey, and captions were written with attention to the time and place of origin as well as the type of object and its use. The more than fifteen hundred color and black-and-white photographs, drawings, and specially designed maps in this set will sharpen readers' skills in assessing the importance of material culture for understanding history. Illustrated feature boxes throughout the set call attention to particularly significant events and themes.

   Each of nine volumes contains its own specialized time line, glossary, bibliography, and index. Volume ten is a treasury of reference information, including a chronicle of world leaders, a panoramic time line of modern world history, a glossary, and a lengthy comprehensive index to nine volumes. In addition, the final volume contains several thematic indexes and an extensive selection of further resources including books, audiovisual sources, historical museums, and a growing number of excellent websites through which primary documents and millions of visual resources can be found.

Contents of Encyclopedia

Origins of the Modern World

The Apostles Peter and Paul Quarreling with Simon Magus in Front of Emperor Nero by Filippino Lippi, fresco, 1481–1483.

CONTENTS

Introduction

Volume 1 of *History of the Modern World* has the ambitious task of setting out the major differences that distinguish the early modern world from the medieval world that preceded it. As the first chapter of this volume, *Origins of the Modern World*, will show, the two periods blend together with no clear break. The political shape of the western world, described in the second chapter, changed only slowly while many elements of medieval life, as explained in chapter three, continued into the modern age. Among those continuing elements was the direct involvement of the vast majority of the world's population in the agriculture on which societies depended for survival.

Among the most important aspects of the coming of the early modern world was the rise of Europe to global prominence. As the final chapters of this volume make clear, however, western Europe was far from the only region undergoing significant developments. Empires were emerging in Russia and Turkey that would come to dominate eastern Europe and the Middle East, respectively. In Africa, trading societies thrived through internal contacts and interchange not only with the Islamic world but also with eastern Asia. In Asia, meanwhile, dynamic empires emerged in India and China that were unrivaled in terms of power and prestige. As the following narrative makes clear, the accomplishments of civilizations around the world made European prominence far from inevitable and yet the dynamic forces released by Europe's internal social, political, and economic changes promoted it eventually to a dominant position on the world stage.

The central sections of this volume explain the impulses that underlay Europe's rise. Increasingly efficient short- and long-range trade encouraged the development of commercial centers and cities and enabled the accumulation of wealth to fund technological developments and cultural endeavors. Those endeavors incorporated varied intellectual traditions. Scholars and artists attempted to establish a framework for assessing their own society by drawing on the legacy of medieval scholasticism and classical learning and formulating a new tradition, humanism. Such developments set the background for the most well-known portent of the early modern world, the artistic flowering in southern and northern Europe called the Renaissance. As the following chapters will show, however, the Renaissance was not entirely a period of enlightenment and accomplishment: despite the spread of humanistic ideals, a legacy of superstition, violence, and poverty remained characteristic of everyday life.

The Editor

Continuity and Change

Old and New in Europe

When the roof of the cathedral of Beauvais in France collapsed in 1284, the townspeople must have wondered if they were part of an ominous pattern of disaster in Europe. By 1194, the cathedral of Chartres in the same country had had to be rebuilt six times. In England, slightly earlier, the cathedral at Old Sarum was destroyed by lightning five days after its consecration; the bishop moved to another town.

In their efforts to produce a magnificent expression of divine glory—the cathedral was to be the largest in Europe—had the people of Beauvais displeased God with a show of pride? In a medieval world in which it was thought that life must be lived entirely in God's service, such an explanation was common for unusual phenomena.

In 1573, the roof of Beauvais Cathedral crashed again, and again many people sought a divine explanation of the catastrophe. Little seemed to have changed in the intervening three centuries. Other people, however, took a more practical view. A collapsing roof, they believed, was as much a human as a divine problem, explicable and solvable without reference to supernatural forces. A largely unobserved but fundamental change had affected Europeans' attitude to their world.

Seeds of Change

From about the fourteenth to the sixteenth centuries, daily life for most people was what it had been for centuries, a series of struggles, from growing food to eat to building structures that would stay up. The majority of people still worked on the same

This present-day view shows Chartres Cathedral in France. The cathedral had to be rebuilt numerous times after it collapsed. Contemporaries saw such misfortunes as signs of God's displeasure, but they had more to do with the shortcomings of contemporary building techniques.

This grinning skull was carved during the fifteenth century in Rouen, in France. It adorned the wall of an ossuary, a place that held the bones of victims of the Black Death.

Famine and Disease

The late medieval period in Europe was a time of fear of disease and famine, and the early modern period saw little improvement. Most people remained vulnerable to innumerable natural or human-made disasters. They relied on the harvest to eat and the weather for the harvest. They had much to be afraid of: famine, predators, storms, drought, blizzards, robbers, unjust trials, and arbitrary punishment. The age-old dread also remained of supernatural spirits who lurked in every shadow.

Disease played an important part in the transition from the medieval to the modern world. In the mid–fourteenth century, a plague called the Black Death struck Europe, killing between a third and a half of the continent's population. The plague left Europe devastated. Fighting ceased for eleven years in the Hundred Years' War between France and England, for example. Farmers could barely plant or harvest their crops. Towns stood deserted.

Effects of the Black Death

The Black Death profoundly undermined European society. The fall in population introduced new movement to the feudal society of the Middle Ages. This system divided society into classes known as estates: the nobility, the clergy, and the peasants. Each estate had obligations to the others. The first estate, the nobility, protected the other two by providing military leadership; the second estate, the clergy—themselves often members of the nobility—maintained the spiritual health of the other two; the third estate, the peasantry, supported society by laboring for their feudal lords.

In return for their obligations, the three estates enjoyed privileges: feudal lords and the clergy were exempt from taxation; lords could also collect revenue from the lands of their vassals, enforce exclusive hunting rights in the forests, and hold their own courts of justice. Free peasants could own land and, along with tenant farmers and villagers, had the right to claim protection and justice from their overlord. Defending these respective privileges was a primary goal of all estates, especially the nobility, who had most to forfeit by losing them.

Even before the Black Death, the feudal system did not entirely reflect the reality of European society. It excluded the very poor, for example, who had no place in the social order. The system also ignored Europe's swelling urban centers. Trade and learning developed after about the twelfth century, but social groups such as acade-

land as their forebears, suffered from the same diseases, and died almost as young.

In other ways, however, Europe was changing. The twelfth, thirteenth, and fourteenth centuries saw a great movement of peasants from the land to the continent's cities, for example. Beneath the apparent continuity of life lay the seeds of Europe's transition from the medieval to the modern world. Developments in politics, religion, society, and trade gradually reshaped the framework of life in Europe and the continent's position in the world. Change was virtually imperceptible.

Life during the European Middle Ages was in many ways quite unlike our lives today. There was only one dominant religion, for example. There were no countries as we know them, with established borders. Centralized government did not exist. Society's structure was based upon a complex system of privileges and duties that were rooted in a world of chivalry and knights in armor.

By the sixteenth century, however, many parts of life had taken on a shape that present-day men and women would find at least partly familiar. Government was becoming more centralized, with bureaucracies and tax collectors. A new emphasis on people's responsibility for their own lives was reflected in sweeping religious reforms. Money was increasingly important in shaping not only the relationships between individuals but also the institutions that dominated society, such as banks and trade guilds.

This fifteenth-century illumination, on a manuscript page so thin that writing shows through from the reverse side, depicts contemporary French noblewomen amusing themselves in a courtyard. Throughout the early modern period, women lacked formal positions in society. Individual women, however, particularly among the nobility, were able to exercise considerable influence, usually through their husbands. Catherine de' Medici, for example, was instrumental in introducing Italian manners and fashion to France after her marriage to King Henry II in 1533.

mics, artisans, and merchants had little part in the traditional estates. Some town dwellers amassed considerable fortunes and political power, yet they remained excluded from the privileges enjoyed by the nobility.

The depopulation that followed the Black Death brought great social mobility. Labor grew scarce, so peasants could sell their services for money to whichever landowner paid most. Other peasants left the land to find employment in the towns, where commerce and education revived and offered increasing opportunities for people to improve their lives.

Humanism

A parallel new emphasis on the individual was also evident in the thinking of a group of scholars and patrons known as human-ists (*see 1:62*). The humanists, who originated in Italy but whose attitudes spread throughout Europe, looked to ancient Rome as a model society. Their emphasis on people and their celebration of worldly pleasures and achievements helped lead Europe away from the medieval view in which human achievement was measured by how much it celebrated God's glory.

In his essay *The Courtier*, the Italian diplomat Baldassare Castiglione (1478–1529) summed up the change in his description of a true gentleman. No longer were piety and spirituality the main virtues. Castiglione's noble was well born and handsome, an expert in warfare, dancing, manners, tennis, music, and art. He was also a poet, able to speak and write Greek and Latin, conversant with Plato and Aristotle, and charming in female company.

This statue of Girolamo Savonarola stands a few miles from the site of his 1498 execution in Florence, Italy. Savonarola's message of piety made him highly popular with Florentine citizens, but he offended the powerful interests of the pope and the aristocracy.

The Value of the Individual

With the new emphasis on the individual came a less fatalistic view of the world. In the late Middle Ages, life expectancy was only twenty-seven years. Infant mortality was high, thanks to the dangers of child-birth and diseases such as tuberculosis. Europeans seem to have accepted such a situation as unalterable. Many historians believe that mothers did not bond with their infants as parents do today, in order to avoid or minimize the emotional devasta-tion of losing children. Such historians argue that the concept of a loving family is a creation of the modern rather than the medieval world.

Because protecting a child from harm was so difficult, many parents did not even try. In townhouses, for example, which often had landings jutting from the upper stories, it was not uncommon for a toddler to crawl out and fall to his or her death in the street below. Such accidents happened so frequently in Geneva, Switzerland, that the religious reformer John Calvin (*see 2:160*) persuaded the council to pass a law requiring householders to erect railings on every landing. The law underlines the new appreciation of the value of human life.

Changes in Religion

Nowhere did the importance of the individ-ual find as much encouragement or have as dramatic an effect as in the changes that swept Christianity in the sixteenth century. In 1517, a monk from Saxony named Martin Luther (1483–1546) protested against various practices of the Roman Catholic Church. Eventually, Luther's action led to the emergence of a new branch of the Christian faith, Protestantism.

The change was momentous. It over-threw the monopoly the Catholic Church had for centuries claimed over the spiritual life of western Europe. Luther's protest, however, was only the latest in a series of challenges to the church's authority.

Throughout the Middle Ages, Cathol-icism was so influential that Europeans defined their continent as Christendom. The word *Europe* itself was barely ever used. In the Byzantine Empire, meanwhile, the Orthodox branch of Christianity was predominant in what are now Greece, the Balkan Peninsula, and parts of Russia.

In the face of the fears and suffering of medieval life, the Catholic Church offered stability to the people and a sense of unity to a fragmented society. The church was the most dependable aspect of ordinary life. Into it one was baptized; within it one received forgiveness; and through it one was assured of eternal life. Security rested in observing the ritual sacraments: baptism, confirmation, the Eucharist, penance, marriage, holy orders, and the last rites.

The village priest was a constant, ministering to several generations of a family, rejoicing or grieving with them, and giving rudimentary education to their children. The church also shaped the calendar. The year was busy with religious festivals such as Epiphany, Lent, Easter, Pentecost, All Saints, Advent, and Christmas, plus about a hundred and fifty other saints' days.

Challenging Church Authority

Throughout the late Middle Ages, reformers challenged the church's spiritual authority. Reformers claimed that it had become too involved in secular concerns. Bishops and popes dabbled in political and military affairs while secular princes asserted their own power against that of the pope, claiming the right to appoint bishops in their own lands, for example. From 1378 to 1417, political squabbles caused the Great Schism, during which two popes simultaneously claimed to lead the church. The episode further weakened Catholicism's claim to spiritual leadership.

Different understandings of some Catholic doctrine—such as how good works and spiritual purity were related to salvation—had differing practical consequences. As early as the tenth century, a revival of biblical study and a life of simplicity were promoted by a new order of monks at Cluny. Some 300 years later, the Dominicans and Franciscans reasserted the need for preaching and for a life of poverty, respectively.

Bernard of Clairvaux (1090–1153), Hildegard, abbess of Bingen (1098–1179), and Thomas à Kempis (c. 1379–1471), author of *The Imitation of Christ*, exalted poverty and a mystical relationship with Christ. Oxford's John Wycliffe (c. 1330–1384) and Prague's Jan Hus (c. 1372–1415), both condemned as heretics, proposed that scriptural teachings take precedence over the authority of the pope (*see 2:152*).

Further Reform

Intent on reforming immorality among churchmen, the Italian monk Savonarola (1452–1498) galvanized Florence for moral renewal. For three years, he virtually ruled the city, condemning the pope and arguing the need to establish an ideal Christian state. Savonarola was unseated, and his denunciation of worldliness eventually brought his martyrdom when he was burned for heresy.

The luxurious lifestyle of Rome continued. Popes Alexander VI, Julius II, and Leo X spent lavishly. The dream of a glorious cathedral—St. Peter's in Rome—prompted Leo X to sell indulgences. These certificates promised the forgiveness of sins for a

The Battle Between Carnival and Lent, painted by Pieter Brueghel the Elder in 1559, shows the citizens of a Flemish town indulging in typical festivities of a Christian holy day. Such regular carnivals relaxed social conventions, helping provide a safety valve for less privileged members of society to get rid of societal tensions.

This nineteenth-century portrait gives an impression of Hugh Capet, who was elected king of France in 987. Capet's descendants proved so adept at centralizing power that they ruled France for some 800 years.

sum of money, seeming to make it possible to buy salvation. It was against the sale of indulgences to build St. Peter's that Martin Luther first protested.

Luther preached salvation by the grace of God rather than by the exercise of good works. Luther's message earned him excommunication from the church, and he barely escaped imprisonment. One part of Luther's doctrine, the priesthood of all believers, cut at the very heart of ecclesiastical power. It taught that each individual is answerable to God and is not sheltered or controlled by the church. Luther urged that people study the Bible for themselves, without using priests as intermediaries. The Reformation Luther began opened the way for a restructured outlook. Both Protestantism and the vigorous Catholic response to it placed their emphasis on the value, responsibility, and potential of each man, woman, and child.

The Reformation did not completely change Europeans' attitude to religion, however. Whether of the Catholic or Protestant branches of the faith, Christianity retained its power over the continent. Religion remained the major force shaping society and the daily lives of Europeans.

The Rise of Royal Power

The fundamental change in the political shape of Europe between the medieval and modern worlds came with the emergence of polities that began to resemble nation-states. This development involved an increasing centralization of power, which itself was both a cause and a result of another distinguishing feature of the early modern world, the rise of monarchy.

Politically, medieval Europe reflected a system that originated with Charlemagne's empire, which had united much of the western continent in the eighth and ninth centuries. Charlemagne split his empire into counties, giving comparatively great power and privileges to local counts in return for loyalty. The relationship of king and duke, like that of lord and peasant, depended on mutual loyalty, based upon a grant of land in exchange for military service and sealed by a ceremony of homage.

The early modern period saw increasing threats to nobles' privileges as monarchs tried to consolidate their power throughout Europe. In 987, for example, the nobles of France elected as king Hugh Capet (c. 938–996) because, as the least powerful among them, he posed little threat to the others. Capet's descendants, however, centralized the power of the monarchy. Louis IX (1214–1270), for whom the American city of St. Louis is named, clarified a standard law code and established a judicial court, the Parlement, that challenged the authority of the nobles' independent courts. Louis's grandson, Philip IV (1268–1314), asserted his authority over church affairs in France and limited the rights of his nobles. In further freeing his rule from constraints, Philip planted the seed of a more powerful monarchy still.

Everywhere in Europe, royal power increased at the expense of the nobility, often in violent conflict between monarchs and their "overmighty subjects." On occasion, however, monarchs were forced to make concessions. In thirteenth-century England, King John granted his barons the right to exercise their privileges in a parliament, a body that, in some cases, could constrain the monarch's power. In Poland-Lithuania, the Jagiello dynasty kept power only by allowing the nobles to establish a similar body, the *sejm*. The power of the nobility in eastern Europe meant that, while the feudal system was disappearing elsewhere, in the

This equestrian statue shows Francis I (1494–1547), king of France. Thanks to the efforts of earlier monarchs, the French kings were some of the strongest in Europe by the time of Francis's reign.

Beynac Castle is a product of the turbulent past of Aquitaine, in France. Having belonged to the kingdom of France, the southwestern province of Aquitaine passed by marriage to England in the twelfth century and was only won back by France at the end of the Hundred Years' War.

This facsimile version of the Magna Carta bears the coats of arms of England's nobles and the royal seals of King John, who signed the original charter in 1215. Although previous kings had granted liberties to their barons, the signing of Magna Carta was the first occasion on which nobles had exacted rights and privileges from a monarch in return for their support.

east it grew stronger as lords imposed vassalage on a previously free peasantry.

In France, England, and, later, Spain, centralized states began to coalesce around rulers. Monarchs' courts attracted nobles; the support of these courtiers, in turn, further increased monarchs' power.

Warfare

The emergence of monarchies coincided with changes in the tactics and weapons of war. In medieval feudal societies, vassals supported lords out of obligations of loyalty. In the fourteenth- and fifteenth-century wars between the city-states of Italy, how-

ever, the competing sides began to hire professional soldiers, or mercenaries. A mercenary would hire himself out to the highest bidder and might fight next year the very duke he had supported this year.

The Hundred Years' War (1337–1457) between France and England, meanwhile, saw the emergence of a sense of national loyalty as a motivating force in warfare. Troops fought for England or France rather than for their lord. Kings still needed to pay their armies, however. Pay required taxation, which in turn, required the approval of parliament in both France and England.

Developments in warfare had effects far beyond the battlefield (*see 1:26*). New weapons undermined the supremacy of the armored knight, on whom feudal society had rested. The Italians used the crossbow, a weapon of deadly accuracy but limited range. The English prevailed over the French in a battle such as Crécy (1346) thanks to the longbow, which could stop cavalry at a distance. Gunpowder, first invented in China, was used from the mid–fourteenth century, although the most effective ways to use gunpowder weapons were not realized for three more centuries, when gunners protected by pikemen became fearsome opponents.

The introduction of professional soldiers and gunpowder weapons made war far more expensive than before. Whoever had the most funds had an advantage on the battlefield. With control of treasuries and taxes, monarchs further increased their centralized power at the expense of nobles, whose own forces usually still depended on feudal ties and methods of fighting.

Changing Trade

From about the twelfth century, Europeans increasingly traded both on their own continent and with other parts of the world (*see 1:40*). The Italian republics of Venice and Genoa, in particular, grew wealthy from commerce with the Near and Far East via the Byzantine and Islamic worlds of the eastern Mediterranean. Great seasonal trading fairs enabled the distribution of commodities within Europe, linking Italy in the south with Germany, the Low Countries, France, and England. In the north, meanwhile, trade in the Baltic was dominated by the Hanseatic League. The league was an economic association that brought together about eighty cities along the North Sea and Baltic coasts to virtually monopolize the commerce of northern Europe.

Improvements in ship design and navigation were encouraging Europeans to venture farther, however. By 1500, it was possible to sail to India and the Americas. A combination of technological innovation and accidents of geography weakened the Mediterranean and Baltic regions. The focus of European commerce shifted north toward the Low Countries as the nations of the Atlantic seaboard—above all Spain, Portugal, England, Flanders, and the Netherlands—became the continent's driving economic powers.

This suit of armor was worn by a German knight around 1500. By that time, gunpowder weapons were making knights largely outdated.

Life in Town

The development of Europe's trade went hand in hand with increased urbanization, particularly in prosperous regions such as northern Italy and Flanders. Established centers of population—Paris, London, Lisbon, Vienna, Zurich, Florence, Rome—maintained their superiority. Newer cities, meanwhile, such as Hamburg, Lübeck, Brussels, Danzig, and Riga, mushroomed thanks to the textile and wine industries, the timber, salt, and metals trades, and the banking industry that accompanied them.

Towns fostered new institutions. One of their distinguishing features was the development of guilds, an early form of labor organization (*see 1:43*). Artisans, craftsmen, and traders formed groups to protect their interests. They set standards of quality, guaranteed prices, and sometimes set wages. The strength of the guilds was a presentiment of the power business would exercise in the modern world. Guild members often ran town governments.

Life in the Country

By far the majority of Europe's population, like that of the rest of the world, was rural (*see 1:29*). Whether the land was worked by serfs, free peasants, or tenant farmers, farming methods were the same. Earlier breakthroughs had significantly increased productivity: the invention of a heavy plow and of harnesses that enabled work animals to pull it and the discovery that clover rebuilds the soil in certain ways made more land productive. An increased amount of food and improved nutrition eventually produced a healthier and larger population in Europe, though not until the eighteenth century.

Europe and the World

The changes that would lead Europe into the modern era had a profound effect on the continent's relative position in the world. In the fifteenth century, it seemed unlikely that the crooked little European peninsula protruding from the Asian landmass would rise to global prominence. A better candidate could be found in China under the Ming dynasty, India under the Moguls (*see 3:407*), or West Africa's wealthy Mali Empire (*see 1:115*).

During the Middle Ages, Europe had been isolated and insular and frequently threatened by invaders from Asia. In the twelfth and thirteenth century, the Mongols of central Asia had ruled western Russia, on Europe's border. Europe also faced a threat from the Muslim Ottoman Turks, who had begun to move westward from their homelands in central Asia in about the twelfth century (*see 1:99*).

Europe's relations with the Muslim world were defined by fear, suspicion, and confrontation. Between the eleventh and thirteenth centuries, for example, the church launched a series of military expeditions, called Crusades, to fight Islamic forces in what is now the Middle East. The Ottomans attacked the 1000-year-old Byzantine Empire, capturing Greece and much of the Balkans. In 1453, the Byzantine capital, Constantinople, now called Istanbul, fell to the forces of Sultan Mehmet.

Brown roofs rise above the reconstructed fifteenth-century seafront of Bergen in Norway. The most important port on Norway's west coast, Bergen fell under the control of German merchants of the Hanseatic League in the fourteenth century, at a time when the league dominated trade in the Baltic region.

Modernity and Progress

The dividing line between the medieval and the early modern world remains inexact. Europeans did not one day suddenly realize that they were living in a new era. Day-to-day life remained little changed: the food on the table, the homes in which people lived, and the work they did were constants.

In identifying the transition between medieval and modern, historians point to numerous elements of more or less gradual change. The existence of change in itself was a symbol of the coming of the modern world. The medieval world had been generally marked by an ideological reluctance to change. A belief that the religious, political, and social order reflected the will of God suggested that change could only have negative effects. In fact, the period from the ninth to the fourteenth centuries had seen gradual but significant change in European society.

In the early modern world, people began to believe that change could be beneficial, although they still remained fearful of possible negative consequences. Even reformers such as Martin Luther believed that change had to be managed within the existing social order. In 1524 and 1525, for example, Luther denounced rioting peasants who looked to him to support their protest against the inequities of German society. The views of a Christian sect called the Anabaptists, who preached that people should obey only the authority of God, not that of earthly rulers, threatened to undermine Europe's political order. They were persecuted by governments and by both the Catholic and Protestant churches.

Humanists such as the great Italian writer Niccolò Machiavelli (*see 1:65*) studied the best ways in which social and political structures might adapt to the new currents of change. The clash between the forces of change and the old, static world of the Middle Ages became a symbol of the early modern age.

Another change that heralded the modern world was the feeling of some Europeans that life was improving. Today, people are accustomed to the idea that in many ways life gets better from generation to generation. Some historians see history as a progress in which the past teaches humanity how to create a better future. The idea of progress, that history is a process of improvement, only really began to emerge in Western thought in the works of the fifteenth-century humanists. It was not a new idea. Christian teaching implies that history has a purpose and that the sufferings of humanity are necessary to lead to salvation. In the eleventh century, the Italian religious thinker Joachim of Fiore proposed that history comprised three ages, those of the Father, which had passed; the Son, in which he was living; and the Holy Spirit, which was to come. Each was an improvement upon the last.

The humanists, however, largely saw history as cyclical rather than linear. Many looked back to ancient Greece and Rome and sought to re-create the achievements of the past rather than improve upon them. Consciousness of coming closer to a return to the golden age, however, did at least introduce the idea of improvement. Europeans were becoming increasingly aware that their ingenuity gave them power over their environment, over their lives, and over structures and institutions of religion, politics, and society that had long seemed unchangeable. That realization, above any other, marked Europe's arrival in the modern world.

A bishop rides on horseback in this detail from a fifteenth-century manuscript. During the sixteenth century, challenges from the Protestant branch of Christianity sparked a reforming movement within Catholicism that replaced the stagnant, worldly church of the late Middle Ages with a more spiritual, adaptable, and reasoned faith better fit to address the early modern age.

A French farmer teaches his son how to plow in this illumination from a thirteenth-century manuscript. Heavy plows like this one only became truly effective with the parallel introduction of harnesses that allowed draft animals to pull them easily.

The psychological shock reverberated throughout Europe. The Byzantine Empire had not only been Europe's buffer against the Islamic world; it was also the last, eastern remnant of the Roman Empire that once covered much of Europe.

In the depths of Christendom's crisis, however, lay the signs of a new, more confident attitude. Barely had Constantinople fallen than merchants from the republic of Venice reappeared in the city's harbor. The thriving trade and competition within Europe made the religion of the Venetians' intermediaries less important than the swift reestablishment of trading routes with the Near and Far East.

Europe Emerges

As Europe was galvanized by thriving trade, religious and political change, and a new spirit of inquiry and adventure, it emerged as the most dynamic of the world's civilizations. Meanwhile, its potential rivals for global power did not move onto the world stage. In Ming China, the dominant philosophy of Confucianism actively discouraged trade, which it ranked as less important than piety. China eventually withdrew from contact with the rest of the world. Mogul India remained similarly insular as its Muslim rulers tried to increase their political control over a great area of the predominantly Hindu subcontinent of Asia. Isolated from the Muslim and Mediterranean worlds by the vast Sahara Desert and the scrubby wilderness of the Sudan, the Mali Empire of western Africa was also weakened by a century of upheaval following changes of leadership.

Within fifty years of the fall of Constantinople, European seafarers had charted their way around Africa to Asia and taken the first steps toward building a trading empire. In the Americas, conquistadores—and the diseases they carried—subdued the civilizations they met and established European primacy.

The discouraged inhabitants of Beauvais, meanwhile, contemplating their collapsed cathedral roof in 1573, were barely touched by such developments. There was no way they could realize that they stood on the brink of a new era, the most prosperous that Europe had ever seen.

The World of Christendom

The Political Shape of Europe

In 1453, Christian Europe faced a crisis. That year, the Muslim Ottoman Turks conquered the city of Constantinople, now called Istanbul. The blow shook Europe. The Ottomans had already overrun much of the Byzantine Empire, which had provided a buffer between Christendom and the world of Islam, by conquering Greece and much of the Balkan Peninsula. Now they had captured Constantinople, the cap-

ital of the Byzantine Empire and of the Orthodox branch of Christianity. The city had great symbolic importance as the last remnant of the great Roman Empire that once bound much of Europe together.

That unity lay in the past. Little now suggested that the states of Europe, squabbling among themselves on a set of peninsulas jutting out of the Eurasian landmass, would rise to global dominance. The Ottomans

Richly gilded in silver, this casket in the shape of a church was used to contain holy relics in the fifteenth century. The Christian faith was one of the most important unifying factors in the emergence of European culture.

19

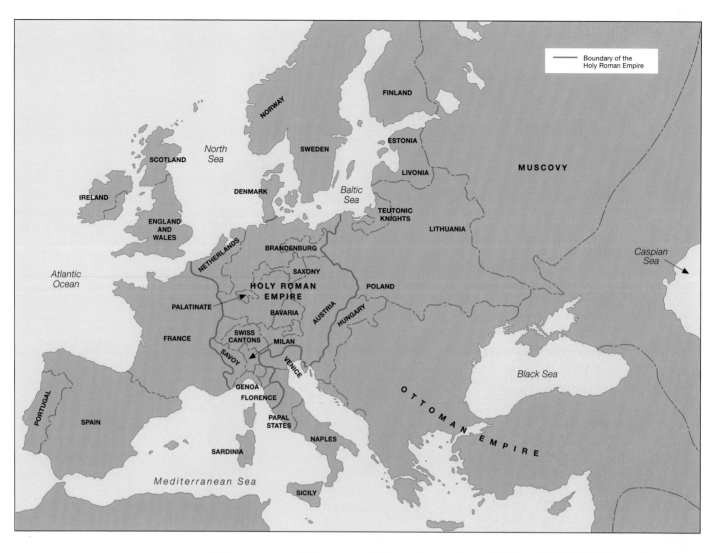

This map shows the main political divisions of Europe in the late fifteenth and early sixteenth century. The Ottoman Empire is shown at its greatest extent in Europe, in about 1560.

would have seemed better candidates in terms of wealth, military power, and the achievements of civilization. So, too, would the Ming of China or the Songhai of West Africa. Within little more than a century, however, Europe would rise to become one of the most powerful regions of the world.

The Decline of Christendom

Around the middle of the fifteenth century, most of Europe's inhabitants had horizons that stretched no further than their village or town or the site of the nearest annual fair. The tiny educated elite perceived Europe not as a geographical but as a religious entity, "Christendom," which united the continent's countries under the symbol of the cross and the authority of God's representative on earth, the pope. The word *Europe* was rarely used.

By 1450, however, the concept of Christendom was on the wane. For thirty years at the end of the fourteenth century, church politics and interference from secular monarchs led to the simultaneous election of two popes, one in Rome and one in the French city of Avignon. This so-called

Great Schism (1387–1417) weakened the authority of the Catholic Church.

A further challenge to papal authority came from the ruler of the Holy Roman Empire. The empire was a collection of German states descended from the empire amassed in the eighth and ninth centuries by one of the greatest of medieval rulers, Charlemagne (742–814). In theory, the Holy Roman emperor was elected by a group of powerful German princes, called electors. In practice, by the mid–fifteenth century, the emperor was always a member of the Austrian Habsburg family.

In spiritual affairs, the empire was subject to the authority of the papacy in Rome, but the emperor was supreme in affairs of the world, called temporal affairs. No clear line divided the spiritual and temporal spheres, however. The pope demanded that the princes of the Holy Roman Empire pay him taxes, for example. The princes, for their part, denied the pope the right to appoint bishops in their domains. The struggle weakened the positions of both pope and emperor.

The early sixteenth century brought the final blows to the idea of Christendom.

First, the German priest Martin Luther sparked the Reformation by challenging the authority of the Catholic Church and establishing a new variant of Christianity, Protestantism (*see 2:151*). Second, since about 1400, Europeans had begun to rediscover the literature, arts, and science of their pre-Christian predecessors, the ancient Greeks and Romans (*see 1:52*). For some historians, the new confidence and spirit of inquiry signaled by this Renaissance—a French word meaning "rebirth"—and the Reformation mark the end of the Middle Ages in Europe and the beginning of the early modern period.

The Idea of Europe

The decline of Christendom saw the rise of the idea of Europe. The concept was both geographical and cultural. It acknowledged that geography united the continent. Questions remained, however. Where did Europe meet Asia in the east? Were the islands of the Mediterranean part of Europe or part of the Muslim world of North Africa? Various considerations helped clarify such issues. Religion was the most important: Europe included not only the Catholics of Christendom but also the Christians of the Eastern Orthodox Church, based first in Constantinople and then in Russia. The two branches of the faith had split in the eleventh century. The distribution of peoples, languages, and culture also played a role in defining the continent. The Mediterranean islands were home to Italian and Spanish speakers, making them part of Europe. Beyond the Volga in Russia, Mon-

Made of stone taken from Rome, Charlemagne's throne still survives in Aachen in Germany. Charlemagne's great medieval empire combined religion and politics in a way that was very influential for future European monarchs.

This coin was minted in Florence in 1478 to celebrate Lorenzo de' Medici's survival of an assassination plot by the conspirators, shown being executed in the lower half of the coin. Violent overthrow was a constant threat to the rulers of even comparatively stable city-states and nations.

goloid rather than Slavic peoples were predominant, making that river the dividing line between Europe and Asia.

The idea of Europe as an entity brought together peoples stretching from Spain and Portugal in the west to the Volga in the east, from the Italian peninsula in the south to Britain and Scandinavia in the north. As a concept, Europe suggested that the different peoples and races of the continent shared more bonds than religion alone.

The Rebirth of Europe
Stirring currents suggested that Europe might recapture some of the dynamism and confidence that characterized the Roman Empire. The twelfth-century rise of universities stimulated the exchange of ideas (*see 1:50*). Trade increased, urban centers encouraged industry, elites emerged to support craftsmen, merchants, and clerks (*see 1:39*). Venice and Genoa in Italy grew prosperous on trade with countries beyond Europe. In the fifteenth century, Europeans looked farther afield to explore Asia and the Americas (*see 3:303*). The new eagerness to find out more about the world marked a new beginning for Europe.

The Shape of Europe
Parts of the map of Europe in the late fifteenth century remain familiar today. The shape of countries such as Spain and

France has changed little. Other elements of the map are almost unrecognizable, however. In what are now Germany and Italy, large nations have replaced a patchwork of smaller states. Elsewhere, the opposite process has seen a host of independent states emerge from a large empire, as in the case of Poland-Lithuania.

Certain trends were common throughout much of Europe. Among the most important effects of the continent's cultural and religious upheavals was a growing sense of national identity. Rather than think of themselves only as citizens of a village or county or as members of the larger Christian community, people began to look upon themselves as members of a nation. They came to think of themselves as English, French, or Spanish, loyal neither to the pope nor to the emperor but to their own national rulers.

Only some of Europe's states developed into what we would call nations, however. In some cases, geography pushed them together, as in Spain. Speaking a common language also bound people into larger aggregates, as again in Spain and also in France. Conquest and defeat, marriages between dynastic families, and military strength or even luck also influenced state development. Smaller states remained liable to fall under the influence of their larger neighbors, as in the case of Scotland and England, Portugal and Spain, or the Low Countries, trapped between the Holy Roman Empire and France. Meanwhile, the German states and the republics of the Italian peninsula, despite sharing their respective common languages and cultures, failed to produce any polities resembling nation-states until centuries later.

The States of Europe
The states of Europe split into various types. In the north and west lay relatively established kingdoms bound together by ethnic and linguistic ties under more or less centralized rule. In the east lay the great, ethnically varied empires of Poland-Lithuania and Muscovy, both of which acted as a buffer between Europe and Asia. It was in the area between these extremes, from the Low Countries in the north through the Holy Roman Empire to the Italian peninsula in the south, that Europe least resembled its current shape.

France
France, England, Spain, Portugal, Denmark, and Sweden were recognizable as early nation-states from their monarchies, capital cities, and more or less centralized

bureaucracies. France was the wealthiest and, with about 12 million people, the most populous nation. France was not entirely united, however. Local nobles retained great influence in fiefs such as Flanders, Brittany, and Burgundy. The Burgundians, in alliance with the English, even controlled Paris from 1418 to 1436. The end of the Hundred Years' War in 1453, a century-long series of occasional English invasions and frequent raids, strengthened Valois power. During the 1450s, the monarchy established increasing control beyond its heartland around Paris. It regained English-held territory along the Atlantic seaboard, apart from the northern port of Calais, and in 1486 acquired Provence in the south and thus a trading presence in the Mediterranean. By the end of the century, France resembled its modern shape.

England

In England, as in France and elsewhere, the late Middle Ages saw the advance of the monarchy over its "overmighty subjects." These feudal chiefs possessed vast tracts of land, supported their own courts, and commanded their own armies of knights. During the fifteenth century, the Lancastrian and Yorkist families fought for the crown. The long struggle—dubbed the Wars of the Roses because both clans took the flower as their symbol—ended in 1485. Henry Tudor, the Lancastrian candidate for the throne, defeated and killed the Yorkist king Richard III at the Battle of Bosworth Field and became the first Tudor monarch (*see 2:205*). The growth of a centralized

monarchy was matched by the development of Parliament, an early medieval assembly of powerful subjects. Monarchy and Parliament became the focuses of national loyalty in England.

Spain

Spain remained divided into distinct kingdoms, including Castile, in the center, whose capital was Madrid, and Aragon in the east. Aragon also ruled the Mediterranean islands of Minorca and Majorca,

A gilt-bronze tomb effigy from 1519 shows England's king Henry VII lying beside his queen, Elizabeth of York. The marriage of the Lancastrian king to a Yorkist princess helped heal the divisions left by the Wars of the Roses.

A relief carved on a Spanish church shows Saint James, Spain's patron saint, crushing the country's Moorish occupiers. The Spanish destroyed the final Moorish state in the Iberian Peninsula in 1492.

The Alcázar, or castle, rises above a shadowed valley in Segovia, in Spain. Built in the fourteenth century and later enlarged, the Alcázar was the fortified castle of the kings of Castile. A number of similar structures were built during the Spanish campaign against the Muslim occupiers; they provided both defense and an impressive display of the power of Spain's own local rulers.

Sicily, Sardinia, and the kingdom of Naples in Italy. In the southern part of the Iberian Peninsula, Granada lay under the rule of Muslims, the Moors of Morocco who had invaded in the eighth century and made Spain the most prosperous and artistically advanced part of Europe.

In 1469, the marriage of Ferdinand of Aragon and Isabella of Castile established the personal union of two kingdoms, though each retained its own parliament and laws. The monarchs imposed a strong unifying force, however. The Inquisition, the ecclesiastical court intended to crush heresy (*see 2:179*), was the first institution with authority throughout their kingdoms.

In 1481, Ferdinand and Isabella launched a campaign against the Moors of Granada, the *reconquista,* or reconquest. They were ultimately successful in 1492 and began driving Muslims and Jews from their enlarged kingdom. It was at this time, too, that Spain, alongside her neighbor, Portugal, took the lead in overseas exploration of the world. Present at the fall of Granada in 1492 was a Genoese seafarer, Christopher Columbus, who was seeking the Spanish monarchs' support for a voyage across the Atlantic.

Scandinavia

In the north, the kingdoms of Denmark, Sweden, and Norway dominated Scandinavia. In 1397, Queen Margaret of Denmark had brought the three into a limited union, reigning in Norway by marriage and in Sweden by election. This Union of Colmar lasted until 1523, when it broke up as a consequence both of war between Sweden and Denmark and of internal conflicts in all three states between the monarchs and the powerful nobles on whom they relied for their election to power.

The union, however, had allowed the kingdoms to begin to weaken the influence of their chief competitor for power in the region, the great trading cartel, the Hanseatic League. This group of Germanic trading towns had since the late thirteenth century controlled the sea trade of the southern Baltic, establishing ports, organizing shipping, and controlling prices. It was only during the Union of Colmar that the Scandinavian powers were able to begin to loosen the league's grip on the region's economy.

The East

In the northeast a new Christian power emerged as the heir of the Byzantine Empire (*see 1:96*). Muscovy had thrown off the rule of the Mongols, who since 1256 had dominated much of Asia. In 1472 the grand duke of Moscow, Ivan, proclaimed himself czar, or emperor, of all Russia. After the fall of Constantinople to the Ottoman Turks, Ivan made Moscow the new capital of the Orthodox Church.

In east central Europe, meanwhile, Poland, Lithuania, Hungary, and Bohemia had long been the subjects of a power struggle between noble dynasties, including the Habsburgs of Austria, who controlled the Holy Roman Empire. In 1386, a marriage united Poland and Lithuania under the Jagiellon dynasty, creating the largest realm in Christendom. The ostensible reason for the union was to fight off the threat of the Teutonic Knights, a band of Germanic warrior-monks. In fact, the union also offered Poland support in its territorial ambitions in the east. For Lithuania, meanwhile, which was still a pagan country, the union brought it into the mainstream of Christendom. Jagiellon rulers also took control of Hungary and Bohemia, in what are now the Czech Republic and Slovakia. Short of money, the Jagiellons made concessions to their nobles to raise support. A parliament, the Sejm, gave the nobles considerable power over the monarchs.

The Jagiellons faced continuing challenges in central Europe from the Habsburg dynasty of Austria. From minor aristocrats, the Habsburgs had grown by virtue of marriages to control an empire that included Austria, much of Burgundy, and what are now the Low Countries. The family also ruled the Holy Roman Empire, whose boundaries overlapped but did not coincide with those of the Habsburg Empire. In their own lands, they were absolute monarchs; in the empire, they were subject to election.

Burgundy and the Low Countries

Among Habsburg possessions, Burgundy had the most illustrious past. The duchy, which included part of northeastern France as well as Flanders and the Netherlands, had, in the thirteenth and fourteenth centuries, been powerful, rich, and a cultural center. After a series of disastrous wars by the Burgundian duke Charles the Bold ended in his defeat and death at the hand of the Swiss in 1476, however, the duchy split apart. The marriage of Charles's daughter, Mary, to Maximilian Habsburg meant that Flanders and the Netherlands passed to the Austrian dynasty. The French monarchs took control of the remainder of Burgundy.

The roots of the duchy's final decline, even in a France where centralized monarchy remained open to challenge, lay in its inability or refusal to join in the new shape of Europe. The loss of the Low Countries removed the duchy's access to the sea and cut off its trade. The duchy also relied on institutions such as the Order of the Golden Fleece, an order of knights that owed more to the chivalric world of the Middle Ages

Cowled monks support a slab bearing an effigy of a Burgundian noble, Philip le Pot, in this tomb built in 1493. By then, the once thriving duchy of Burgundy had been split between the Austrian Habsburgs and the French. As Grand Seneschal, Philip administered France's Burgundian possessions on behalf of the monarch.

Armies, Weapons, and Warfare

In 1476, a Swiss army mainly composed of infantry wielding pikes, axes, and two-handed swords defeated Charles of Burgundy at the Battle of Murten. The defeat marked the end of the duchy of Burgundy as a major force in Europe. It also confirmed the emergence of Switzerland as an important power. During the fourteenth century, a number of Swiss cities and cantons, or counties, allied together to establish independence from the German Empire. With each military victory, more cantons joined the Everlasting League, as Switzerland was then known. Military victory and successful state building were directly linked, and the emergence of Switzerland confirmed the Swiss as the best soldiers in Europe. Swiss troops were in great demand as mercenaries for other armies. The Swiss Guards who still guard the pope in the Vatican date from 1516.

Warfare was endemic in Europe. Not only did states fight one another; within states, dynasties fought for political power. In the Italian Peninsula, city-states constantly warred for territory or trade. The constant warring was one reason Europe remained relatively weak at the beginning of the early modern period. No such internal upheavals weakened the Ottoman Empire, for example.

Though endemic, European warfare remained limited. Tiny armies fought, regrouped, and fought again. Attacks usually targeted strongpoints or castles rather than enemy armies. Armored cavalry, descended from chivalric knights, were the backbone of virtually all armies. The infantry—usually peasants supplied by feudal lords—were ill disciplined and more interested in pillage than in victory.

In the fourteenth and fifteenth centuries, things began to change. Among the warring city-states of Italy, it became common to supplement armies with *condottiere*, or professional mercenary soldiers. In cases such as that of Milan, *condottiere* commanders took control of the very states that had employed them.

Weapons changed, too. Technological improvements gave both the longbow and the crossbow increased firepower. More important, the spread of gunpowder in Europe during the fourteenth century—it had been introduced from China a century earlier—saw the emergence of artillery and, more slowly, firearms.

Still, warfare remained uncharacterized by considerations—such as national loyalty—that later became important. Just as mercenaries fought for whoever paid them, advancements in technology became available to whoever wished to buy them. When the Ottoman Turks overthrew Constantinople in 1453, they used seventy artillery guns to bombard the city. The Ottoman artillery maker was a Hungarian Christian named Urban. Urban had offered his services to the Byzantines in Constantinople, but they could not raise his fee. Urban therefore sold his expertise to the Ottoman sultan Mehmed II.

The growth of artillery had profound effects. It rendered existing fortifications obsolete. They had been built as tall as possible to avoid being scaled. Now, architects designed lower, thicker walls to withstand the impact of cannonballs.

On the battlefield, firearms remained a small but growing part of the armory. The 1450s saw the introduction of the arquebus, a primitive handgun fired by a match. Although it was slow to load and limited in its range, the arquebus, unlike the longbow, whose archers needed strong forearms, required little training for use. At first, however, firearms were typically used to protect the main infantry, which usually carried pikes. In 1534, the Spanish reversed the roles, using pikes to protect the more effective guns.

Such changes had an impact on warfare in general. Professional armies, new weapons, and the extraction of minerals and making of gunpowder made waging

This manuscript illustration from around 1400 shows a soldier manning a gun emplacement. Such early artillery pieces rapidly developed into large guns such as those that bombarded Constantinople only fifty years later, one of which had a range of over a mile.

Soldiers in the army of the Habsburg emperor Maximilian fire various types of guns in this painting from 1505. At the bottom of the page, a soldier supports a three-barreled arquebus on a handheld rest. The matchlock in the center of the gun held the slow-burning match that fired the weapon.

war more expensive. Whereas feudal lords had been able to raise and arm military companies relatively easily from among their peasants, now the strongest armies could be raised by those with access to the most cash. Control of the treasury or tax-gathering powers was as important as feudal or national loyalty in determining the strength of an army. This, in turn, gave monarchs who had a degree of centralized control an advantage over nobles who might potentially challenge them. In the new age of warfare, only the wealthy could wage war.

Battlements and towers still surround the Italian town of Montagnana, near Padua. Such defenses were common in fifteenth-century Italy because of the frequent wars between rival city-states.

than to the emerging new world of universities, bureaucracies, and trade.

The Low Countries, meanwhile—what are now Belgium and the Netherlands—embraced the new world order. While Flanders became prosperous and urbanized, thanks largely to its wool trade with England, the Netherlands became a major shipping power. Economic health promoted cultural vigor and placed the Dutch in position to throw off their Habsburg rulers in the next century (*see 2:215*).

The Italian Peninsula

Despite its common language and its heritage as the heart of the Roman Empire, the Italian peninsula had no political unity. No real idea of Italy existed among Italian speakers. Italy was broken up among a number of self-ruling cities, called city-states, and the Spanish kingdom of Naples. Naples covered the southern half of the Italian peninsula but was too sparsely populated to be politically powerful, with hardly more than a million inhabitants.

Italy in the fourteenth and fifteenth centuries was marked by constant struggles for supremacy among the city-states. The most important were the republic of Venice, with a million inhabitants throughout its territory; the duchy of Milan, which was about the same size but lacked the wealth and artistic brilliance of Venice; and, smaller than both, Florence. Under the Medici, Florence was the leading cultural center in Europe and was home to many of the great achievements of the artistic Renaissance (*see 1:80*). Pisa and Genoa, meanwhile, were prosperous maritime powers. Even

the smallest of the Italian city-states clung tenaciously to their liberty. The republic of San Marino and the principality of Monaco remain nominally independent today.

Each city-state had its own form of government. There was no general pattern. Since the tenth century, Venice, for example, had been ruled by a doge, or leader, who was elected for life. Milan, meanwhile, was ruled by the Sforza family. The Sforzas built up a strong army to protect their interests and posted civil servants throughout the peninsula to govern their possessions beyond Milan.

The Holy Roman Empire

The Holy Roman Empire, like Italy, comprised numerous principalities, ranging from large, relatively powerful states, such as Saxony, to independent towns, such as Nuremburg, whose citizens vigorously asserted their freedom from aristocratic rule. Each principality looked after its own affairs, but they all shared a nominal allegiance to the emperor. The emperor's power had been weakened, however, by his struggles against the pope. By the early sixteenth century, the rulers of some more powerful German states were prepared openly to challenge the emperor. Their ambition would help fuel the spread of Protestantism as they joined their temporal ambitions to the religious reforms of the Reformation. The Reformation began in the German city of Wittenberg in 1521, and it was among the turbulent politics of the Holy Roman Empire that the new faith of Martin Luther was to find its earliest foothold (*see 2:154*).

Population and Agriculture

Supporting the Continent's Citizens

One of the major factors behind social and economic developments in early modern Europe was population change, which itself reflected the continent's ability to feed its citizens As it had been during the Middle Ages, early modern Europe was a largely agricultural continent. In this it resembled every other major contemporary civilization. Despite the growth of towns and cities, the vast majority of people lived in the countryside. They either worked on the land or in small-scale industry directly connected to agriculture, such as weaving, dyeing, or brewing.

Agriculture shaped life. The rhythms of daily life were dictated by the seasons and

This elaborate Flemish book illustration from about 1513 shows the summer harvest in May or June. Men and women labor together just outside the town whose citizens depend on a successful harvest to see them through the year.

29

This Swiss illumination from the first half of the fourteenth century shows a young, noble couple dancing. Because they did not have to work to achieve financial independence, the nobility often married younger than the majority of the population.

Mediterranean and Constantinople, today called Istanbul, in 1347. Its progress was rapid. It reached Italy, Spain, and France in 1348 and Switzerland, Austria, Germany, the Low Countries, and England only a year later. In 1350, it arrived in Scandinavia and Poland. The disease devastated Europe's population and economy. Some regions lost up to 60 percent of their population. Historians estimate that Europe's total population fell by about 40 percent between 1348 and 1377.

Effects of the Black Death

The effects of the plague were felt most in towns where high numbers of people lived in close proximity and the disease spread rapidly. Rural areas also suffered, however. The drastic fall in population created a shortage of labor. Marginal lands—such as foothills, the edges of moorland, or forest fringes that required a lot of labor to become agriculturally productive—were deserted. Mobility among the peasantry increased as they sought food and livelihoods elsewhere. As a result, landlords had to compete for new tenants. Such developments contributed to the loosening of the traditional feudal ties between lord and peasant, in which a peasant labored for a lord in return for protection and the right to farm some of the lord's estate.

Europe took a long time to recover from the Black Death. For most of the fifteenth century, the population remained static or declined. Prices, commerce, and industrial and agricultural production declined or stagnated. A decline in consumer demand caused a widespread depression. Agricultural prices and income fell, so the rural poor had less money to buy anything but staples, such as bread. Artisans and craftsmen lost work as demand fell for their goods, whose price remained relatively high.

The depression ended between 1460 and 1500. By around 1500, too, Europe's population had begun to recover, albeit slowly at first. In the period from 1560 to 1589, England's population increased by about 1 per cent annually. Between 1500 and 1700, the continent's population nearly doubled, from 80 million to around 150 million.

Sources and Figures

The study of preindustrial populations is challenging for historians because of a lack of official records and censuses. In England, for example, a national census, or population count, was not introduced until 1801. In 1538, however, the privy councillor Thomas Cromwell decreed that England's parish priests should keep regis-

the harvest. Even lawyers and academics from the towns would return to the country to help with the harvest. It was vital that they did so: growing enough food to last the winter was the primary concern of any community. Most of the population lived at a subsistence level.

Agriculture closely affected Europe's population. The amount of food available dictated how many people the continent could support. Crop failure brought starvation and diseases stemming from malnutrition. Periodic famine resulted when there was not enough food to go around, laying waste the population.

The Black Death

Along with the food supply, the major influence on Europe's population figures was disease. In the fourteenth century, the continent suffered from the Black Death. This plague, spread by fleas carried on black rats, first reached the eastern

ters noting baptisms, burials, and marriages within their parishes. Similar records were widely kept throughout Europe, and it is by piecing these together that historians deduce population levels in early modern Europe. Their figures are estimates, however, as gaps remain in the record.

Parish registers across Europe confirm that the continent's population was rising in the late sixteenth and early seventeenth centuries. The population rose in Germany, Spain, Italy, the Netherlands, and England. In the principality of Osnabruck in western Germany, for example, the population grew by over 80 percent. The rural populations of the kingdom of Naples, Sicily, Sardinia, and the Swiss canton of Zurich doubled over a hundred years.

Historians estimate that the English population had probably regained the level at which it stood before the 1348 Black Death by 1570. By 1600, it stood at between 4 and 4.5 million. France's population was about the same in 1562 as it had been 250 years earlier. The long series of civil wars called the Wars of Religion (*see 2:195*) combined with plague and other diseases to

slow recovery. Nonetheless, France remained the largest nation-state of early modern Europe.

Marriage and the Birthrate

Historians used to stress the difficult and short lives common in the early modern period. Life expectancy at birth in about

This nineteenth-century illustration shows a black rat, the animal that spread the Black Death across Europe.

A relief carved around 1340 by Andrea Pisano for the cathedral in Florence, Italy, shows a doctor treating patients. Without an understanding of the causes of diseases, such as the plague, or of complications in childbirth, there was little that contemporary medicine could do to reduce Europe's mortality rate.

This French print from the sixteenth century shows a silver mine in operation. Mining increased throughout Europe thanks to technological developments, an increased demand for minerals—partly for minting money—and the availability of a larger workforce.

1500 was 41.68 years, however. Although this does not seem very high today, it was actually higher than in any historical period before the great modernization of the late nineteenth century. People also tended to marry later than historians previously thought, contributing to the population's slow recovery from the Black Death.

In the first half of the seventeenth century in England, the age of first marriage for men was twenty-eight; for women it was twenty-six. This late age of first marriage was typical of preindustrial Europe. People were reluctant to marry before they had an adequate means of supporting a family. They also remarried quickly if a partner died, because marriages were economic partnerships. Late marriages limited population growth, because single women could not legitimately bear children. Having children outside marriage was frowned upon by the church, which served as a powerful social control. Stillbirths were relatively common due to the malnu-

trition of the mother. Infant mortality was also high, due to disease and the poor nutrition of both mother and infant. Overall, the mortality rate was generally high and could always be made worse by disease or famine. In England, the normal death rate was about 30 per 1,000 annually, but it could rise three or four times as high after a failed harvest or an outbreak of disease.

The Threat of Famine

Preindustrial Europe was highly susceptible to crop failure. A bad harvest could easily push large numbers of people below the subsistence line into starvation or leave them ill nourished and vulnerable to disease. Crop failure and subsequent famine inevitably resulted from bad weather.

A series of wet, cold summers could have a disastrous cumulative effect. The study of tree rings reveals bouts of prolonged bad weather and poor growing seasons in the 1590s, 1620s, and 1640s. The papers of estate managers and records of the payment of tithes—taxes paid by peasants to the church—from many areas confirm a reduction in crop yields.

In the second half of the seventeenth century, Europe suffered what historians call the Little Ice Age. Summer temperatures dropped by about one degree centigrade. This drop may not sound like much, but it had a severe impact on the grain harvest. Agricultural techniques were still too primitive to increase productivity. The growth of the population had brought large amounts of marginal land back under cultivation, and crops here were particularly susceptible to the effects of cooler weather.

Cereals and Hunger

Europe's population largely depended on cereals as their basic food. Staples such as potatoes and rice had barely been introduced to the continent (*see 3:392*). If the grain harvest failed, bread prices soared to a level beyond the reach of most poor families. By the early 1600s, wheat cost approximately five times more than it had in the late 1400s. Famine caused heavy mortality in the 1550s, the late 1590s, the 1620s, between 1648 and 1652, and in the 1690s and 1720s. Hunger caused suffering in many other years, but after really bad harvests, people starved to death. Many others died of disease or food poisoning after eating inferior or rotten food. Hunger itself also weakened resistance to disease, which the medical profession could do little to stop. Despite such setbacks, the population of Europe continued to climb until about 1700.

Industry and Urbanization

Europe's expanding population after 1500 brought an expansion of industry. Mining increased, and the amount of iron, copper, and silver extracted from Europe's mines quadrupled. In the sixteenth century, the spread of book printing stimulated older industries, such as papermaking. Although industry often took place in the countryside, it also encouraged the emergence of cities, which grew much faster than the overall population. London had 50,000 inhabitants in the early sixteenth century. A hundred years later, its population was more than 200,000. The increasing urban population encouraged civic building. Much of Rome as it survives today was built in the sixteenth century.

An early sixteenth-century illustration from a Flemish workshop shows reapers and sheepshearers working in July. Throughout much of Europe, sheep raising required increasing amounts of land.

This sixteenth-century woodcut shows a man preparing parchment to be used for bookbinding. Parchment, made from animal hide, was often used to bind the earliest printed books.

Painted by the famous Dutch painter Hieronymus Bosch (c. 1450–c. 1516), *The Prodigal Son* gives a good impression of the appearance of a vagabond in the early sixteenth century. The man carries his belongings in a wicker basket and has a knife, both for protection and to eat with.

Decline of Feudalism

Across western Europe, the feudal system that tied peasants to the land and lords and peasants to each other in a system of mutual obligation had begun to break down, partly as a consequence of the Black Death. Under feudalism, serfs were obliged to work the demesne, or home farm, of their lord in exchange for protection and the right to work a part of their lord's land for their own food.

The system came under threat from economic changes. During the fifteenth and sixteenth centuries, the use of money rather than barter became increasingly common in Europe. Nobles and lords began to buy more commodities from merchants and craftsmen than in the past, so they needed to raise money. They began to exchange some of the traditional dues and services owed to them for money by leasing their estates to raise cash rents. Leasing was not the only means by which landlords adapted to a money economy. The profits that could be made through raising sheep for the growing wool industry lured many land-lords into evicting their tenants to farm their whole estate themselves commercially with hired labor.

Where demesne farming declined, serfdom lost its economic importance. Landlords might offer their serfs their freedom in exchange for a fee. Peasants did not always get the better end of the bargain, however. They lost the feudal contracts that promised protection and a subsistence living in return for labor. A new class of agricultural laborer was born, dependent on wage labor and the market economy—and more vulnerable to recession.

Enclosing the Land

The sixteenth century witnessed the first wave of enclosures in Europe. The process was most marked in England, where many landowners put up fences around common lands that were traditionally open to all the animals of the locality. The land was thus reserved exclusively for the landowners' own crops or sheep. Historians estimate that about one-eighth of England's fertile land was enclosed by 1600. The decisive

had generally been hereditary and rents fixed. The new princelings upset the system to enforce heavy taxes on their tenants to support their own lifestyles.

Peasant Unrest

The sixteenth century was an age of permanent agrarian unrest as the peasants resisted the dues and services that their landlords tried to enforce. Occasionally, peasant resistance erupted into rebellion and violence toward tax collectors, nobles, or food suppliers. There were minor peasant movements in England, while from the mid–sixteenth century, peasant uprisings occurred almost annually in regions across France. Modern Germany saw the greatest

This German woodcut from 1483 shows peasants carrying bundles of wood. The right to gather wood for building or for fuel was one of the feudal rights that landlords increasingly denied their peasants.

factor favoring land enclosure in England was the expanding manufacture of woolen textiles, particularly in the Low Countries.

The demand for wool was a powerful lure for landlords to increase their revenues by raising sheep. Landlords took over common land, consolidated the scattered strips of land cultivated by villagers and enclosed them with hawthorn hedges, and converted various small peasant holdings into large farms. Arable land formerly used for crops became pasture for sheep. Hereditary tenants were evicted, and landowners cultivated their holdings themselves.

Eastern Europe

The general effect of enclosure in western Europe was to weaken, if not destroy, the old feudal system. In the east, meanwhile, the effect was the opposite. Increasingly reliable transport, usually by water, made it possible for the Baltic lands to export grain on a large scale to northwestern Europe. In order to achieve efficiency, the nobles—who were granted considerable power by the region's relatively weak monarchs—imposed serfdom on a peasantry that had previously enjoyed considerable freedom.

Peasants suffered in western Europe, too. As prices rose throughout the sixteenth century, landlords enforced every claim they possessed over the peasantry. In southwestern Germany, for example, landlords grew so powerful that they virtually became tiny sovereign princelings of their lands. In Germany, as in France, tenures

A page from a richly decorated book of hours from 1416 shows laborers working in the fields around a French town in early spring. Books of hours contained information about the calendar and the appropriate religious observances for particular seasons and times. This book was illustrated by the Limburg brothers for the Duke de Berry.

35

This early-fourteenth-century book illustration shows a Swiss prince distributing alms to the sick and disabled. Even the so-called deserving poor depended largely on private rather than public charity for their survival.

many turned to begging and vagrancy. Some ended up in towns, seeking to earn a livelihood through industry and trade. Many who could not find work turned to crime, which became a serious problem in the sixteenth century. In England, the constant migration of large numbers of vagrants from town to town gave rise to a belief that the country was overpopulated.

The local elite who traditionally enforced social discipline could no longer restrain potential troublemakers. They had lost most of their influence with the decline of feudalism. They had also lost power by becoming themselves dependent on the market economy.

Attitudes to the Poor

Poverty was a common condition in the early modern period. Europeans saw the poor as comprising two groups. The honest poor, such as the disabled, lacked property and income through no fault of their own and deserved some assistance. The much larger class of undeserving poor comprised the beggars and vagabonds who simply refused to work.

London had twelve times as many beggars in 1594 as in 1517, although the city's population had barely quadrupled. In Lyons in France, 75 percent of the population was too poor to pay taxes. Contemporaries deplored extreme poverty, but they were less concerned with solving the problem than with the disorder and potential social unrest it represented.

Town and Country

Vagrancy was only one symptom of urbanization. Major differences developed between life in the country and life in the town. Although rural conditions could be harsh, peasants escaped the worst suffering of the urban poor. Crime and plagues were much more serious in towns. Unlike the upper classes, who fled to the country at the first sign of disease, the poorer classes had no choice but to remain. Famine was also more devastating in towns because of poor sanitation and remoteness from food supplies. The urban dweller had no option of growing his or her own food.

The towns were focuses of industry and trade, but these were not wholly urban phenomena. The wool industry in particular was rooted largely in rural areas. Peasants took on additional work when their work in the fields allowed them time. Weaving and spinning, which were traditionally done by women, earned money and brought greater independence from famine. Women were valued economic partners in a marriage.

unrest: there were eleven major uprisings between the early fifteenth century and the great peasant revolt of 1525 and 1526.

Inflation and Crime

Europe's landowners and food producers benefited from the inflation of the sixteenth century, triggered partly by the introduction of precious metals from the New World (*see 3:388*). Some people amassed great wealth. Tenant farmers benefited, because rents rose more slowly than food prices. Laborers suffered, because wages did not keep pace with inflation. One historian estimates that, by about 1600, a laborer's income had about half the purchasing power of a century earlier. The most drastic impact of this came in eastern Europe, where laborers were forced back into serfdom.

In western Europe, where large numbers of peasants were displaced by enclosure,

This engraving shows the German city of Cologne in about 1493. In the background, a crane testifies to a civic building program sponsored by the town's wealthy urban elite.

The textile industry linked town and country through the "putting-out system." Entrepreneurs, usually urban merchants, judged the market, accumulated raw materials that they sent to rural workers to process, then collected and sold the result.

The Character of the Town

The early modern town was defined not merely by the size of its population but by its density. Even if a town's inhabitants numbered only a few thousand, their proximity prompted the evolution of sophisticated political and administrative structures. These structures were dominated by an elite who celebrated their position through civic rituals. They also contributed to municipal building projects, churches, gardens, and other collective schemes for the improvement of towns.

Towns served as magnets for cultural exchange and production. Gradually, cities began to dominate the economic and social life of Europe. This dominance did not reflect only the growing urban population. It stemmed also from broader economic, social, and cultural changes in the sixteenth and seventeenth centuries.

The major factors in the process included the extension of landlords' power through

This contemporary miniature shows shops in a town in France in the fifteenth century. As towns grew, so permanent stores increasingly replaced temporary markets as the chief places to buy supplies.

enclosure and the growth of rural industry controlled by urban entrepreneurs. Other factors included the expansion of the state and its administration, which was dominated by urban elites, and the movement to the cities of many nobles, particularly in France. Cities became associated with refinement and culture. They also served as marriage markets for a member of the elite seeking an eligible partner.

Paris's growth was particularly linked to this trend. The French capital became the center of noble residence and elite culture until the Palace of Versailles, outside the city, became the royal center in the seventeenth century. Any ambitious noble was attracted to the court.

Changing Fortunes

Despite widespread poverty, some people had the chance to improve their status in the early modern period through the eco-nomic opportunities offered by rising industrial production, administrative expansion, and the growth of trade. Fortunes were made and titles were won at courts, in royal administrations, in law, in the growing cities, and overseas in expanding empires. New noble dynasties began as men made their fortunes and assumed an aristocratic lifestyle.

England's wealthy increased their influence by buying land that had been confiscated from monasteries after England split from the Catholic Church. France sold government offices to raise revenue and build the bureaucracy. In return for cash, kings in Spain also sacrificed some control over the appointment of financial and judicial offices. The New World gave minor Spanish nobles the chance to acquire immense estates. By the 1620s, a new aristocracy had emerged that was destined to dominate Europe for centuries.

Trade and Wealth

The Economic Basis of Social Change

The emergence of the modern world in the fifteenth and sixteenth centuries and the European cultural flowering known as the Renaissance were made possible by the wealth of the continent. Since the twelfth century, trade and commerce had been generating more money in Europe than ever before. The patrons who hired artists, collected books, and built churches and palaces had money to invest. Often they celebrated their material possessions by having artists include expensive artifacts, furniture, and cloth in the backgrounds of the paintings they commissioned.

Such an attitude marked a great change from the outlook of the Middle Ages. Then, church leaders had condemned the accumulation of wealth as a symptom of plac-

The Flemish artist Quentin Massys painted *The Tax Collector* in 1539. In order to pay its taxes, the family has brought not only the money on the table but also a chicken.

39

Built in the late Middle Ages in Auvillar, France, this covered hall—a structure built to shelter and accommodate traders—was the site of the town's regular market.

ing material considerations higher than spiritual ones. Europe's nobility had also viewed trade as an unworthy pursuit.

Early modern Europeans' celebration of wealth also marked them out from their contemporaries in other societies. In China, for example, the Confucian religion condemned trade, and merchants belonged to the lowest classes of society. Like China, the Ottoman Empire had few internal trade centers but granted lucrative concessions to foreign merchants. Some economists argue that Europe's many competing currencies, traders, and markets stimulated the economy and gave people the impulse to become involved in international trade (*see 3:295*)

Inheritance from the Past

Economic developments did not mark a sudden or complete break with the past. Most change was gradual and preserved a large degree of continuity with the medieval world. The economy remained dominated by agriculture. Some 80 percent of Europeans still lived in villages and worked on the land, raising crops or livestock. Virtually everyone else either traded agricultural produce or worked in home-based industries founded upon agriculture, such as weaving, brewing, and dyeing.

From around the twelfth century, however, the growth of Europe's towns and, later, the emergence of centralized bureaucracies began to create a powerful minority of craftsmen, lawyers, and scholars who lived in towns and sometimes had little contact with the land. Europe's old universities, such as Oxford in England, divided the year into semesters shaped by the need for students to help with the harvest.

Urbanization was itself prompted by industry and trade. Flanders, in Belgium, became more urbanized as workshops grew up to treat raw wool imported from England, mainly via the port of Antwerp.

Markets and Fairs

The main places where people exchanged goods remained, as in the Middle Ages, markets and trading fairs. Permanent stores, as we know them today, were rare. Markets, held once or twice a week, allowed agricultural producers to exchange produce or sell it to townspeople. In some places, permanent structures accommodated the market, as in the buildings called halles in French towns.

The less frequent, seasonal trading fairs were much larger than markets. For weeks at a time, they took on the appearance of temporary towns as traders set up stalls, merchants held meetings, and visitors enjoyed the unaccustomed crowds and variety. Fairs, such as that held in Champagne in northeastern France, were important in linking northern and southern Europe. Short journeys from fair to fair, for example, were how English wool passed to weavers in Italy. Fairs provided a forum for the exchange not only of goods but also of ideas and cultural developments.

Trading Networks and Powers

Seasonal fairs were the focal points of trade networks that linked Europe and the world beyond. The countries of Scandinavia produced timber, fish, and flax; English wool formed the basis of the woollen industry of the Low Countries and Italy; German minerals spread widely, as did the books that originally came from German printing presses. As the nobles of eastern Europe and the Baltic imposed a feudal system on previously free peasants, they began to ship cheap grain to the rest of Europe.

Europe's cities looked to trade to secure an advantage over their rivals. In northern Europe, the Hanseatic League emerged in the late Middle Ages as a trade network of some 150 towns, mainly in what is now eastern Germany. The league exercised a virtual monopoly over trade in the Baltic region and traded overland deep into what is now Russia. The towns of the league were usually free towns, independent of the rule of princes and aristocrats and dominated by powerful merchants. By 1500, the league's influence was declining as other powers challenged its status. The English and, particularly, the Dutch became northern Europe's dominant shippers.

The Wider World

Enterprising trading centers increasingly linked Europe to the wider world. Merchants from the great maritime republics of Venice and Genoa traded with the Islamic world of northern Africa and the Levant, which we now call the Middle East. The Venetians, in particular, were the intermediaries in trade between Europe and the Far East via the Byzantine and Ottoman empires. Merchants imported silks from as far away as China and spices from India and the islands of Southeast Asia. Venetian merchants were the byword of practicality. When the Ottomans captured the Byzantine capital, Constantinople, in 1453, Venetian merchants returned to the city the next

year to establish their trading privileges. Venice itself became one of the most splendid and opulent of all Renaissance cities.

The Portuguese discovery just before 1500 of a sea route around Africa to India and the Spice Islands damaged Venetian trade. When Spain began to exploit the plantations and mines of its colonies in the New World, the focus of Europe's maritime trade shifted from the eastern Mediterranean to the Atlantic seaboard. There, in

This manuscript illustration shows Venice in the fourteenth century. The city grew rich thanks to its maritime trade.

Europeans in East Asia barter for goods in this engraving from 1555. Such goods might end up anywhere in Europe, carried along the extensive trade networks that crossed the continent.

the north, the Dutch developed the flyboat, a quick, deep-hulled vessel for transporting bulk goods. The discovery went part way toward overcoming a persistent problem facing Europe's economic growth—the difficulty of long-distance transport.

Obstacles to Trade

Transport was only one of the problems restricting European trade. In general, there was relatively little coinage in sixteenth-century Europe, though it increased as mineral extraction gave the continent more metal. Sweden, for example, relied on such medieval means of trading as barter and exchange until it began to mine copper and mint coins late in the sixteenth century. In other parts of the continent, where local rulers minted their own coins, an unregulated system of different currencies made life difficult for traders. On a relatively short journey around the Low Countries in about 1520, the artist Albrecht Dürer had to

This copy of a fifteenth-century image painted on a cathedral window in France shows travelers paying tolls to cross a bridge. Tolls and customs barriers added substantial costs to trade.

The town hall of Lübeck, in northern Germany. Lübeck prospered as the headquarters of the Hanseatic League from 1358 to 1630, when the league was dissolved.

deal in eighteen separate currencies, including English anglots, German pfennigs, Portuguese gulden, and Hungarian ducats.

It was not only proliferation that made coinage inconvenient. Coins were heavy, and transporting them, like transporting most goods, was slow and unreliable. Land transport remained limited by poor roads that were unpassable in winter, by the lack of strong draft animals—the horse and the mule were the most common—and by the threat of brigandage and robbery. Transport by river or sea was more reliable and more common. It remained vulnerable to bad weather and piracy, however, and was often slow. Grain imported from the Baltic in the 1590s was a year old by the time it reached the Mediterranean countries.

Tolls and Towns

Traders faced a restrictive level and number of tolls and duties. Parts of Europe comprised many small principalities, all of which imposed tolls on goods passing through. In the late sixteenth century, the Elbe River had thirty-five customs posts; in France, the Loire had more than 200 tolls. A merchant on a short journey from Basel in Switzerland to Cologne in Germany noted thirty-one customs barriers. Such costs drastically cut merchants' profits. Sea trade was more profitable because it avoided tolls. Spanish merchants importing goods from Asia and the New World sent them north to the port of Antwerp, in modern Belgium, for distribution in northern Europe. Shipping cargos by sea could yield profits of 100 percent on the journey.

This contemporary watercolor shows a Venetian banker counting money in the sixteenth century. The safe beside him contains large bags of coins.

The Guilds

Control of trade in Europe's towns, meanwhile, often rested with guilds. These professional unions united craftsmen or workers in a certain field, such as weaving, and controlled all aspects of their business. They regulated apprenticeships, trading licenses, the quality of goods, and wages and prices. The guilds played an important role in guaranteeing the professionalism and income of their members.

Guilds were also an inherently conservative force. They created urban elites who jealously guarded their own positions at the expense of others. As the rising population of the sixteenth century brought more and more people to towns to earn a living,

guilds reacted by barring new members from their profession. In Liège, in 1589, the cloth guild forbade the introduction of a new type of loom that would allow weavers to produce more work, claiming that it was protecting the livelihood of poor weavers.

Encouraging Change

By the late sixteenth century, however, the guilds were already symbols of the past. Europe's economy was changing. This change was partly the consequence of the breakdown of the feudal structure of society. The mid-fourteenth-century plague called the Black Death killed up to a third of Europe's population, creating large amounts of cheap land and available capital. Ties between peasant and lord that had depended on dues of labor and loyalty increasingly gave way to relationships based on money wages. Food prices fell, leaving people with more income to buy manufactured goods, diverting money into the pockets of urban manufacturers and traders. Towns grew in size and power: by 1500, Europe possessed some 150 towns numbering more than 10,000 inhabitants.

These urban centers offered attractive opportunities for merchants, who, rather than traveling around, increasingly worked in shops and administered their business through agents connected by mail. Since medieval times, merchants who had accumulated savings had advanced money to others to finance investment schemes. These so-called merchant bankers came into conflict with the Catholic Church, which banned usury, or charging interest on loans. The church argued that interest was a sin, because it represented profit for

A golden model of a flyboat stands above the gable of a house that once belonged to a powerful merchant guild in Antwerp, Belgium. The crest celebrates the source of the city's wealth as Europe's leading port.

no labor. Early bankers and moneylenders adopted various means to overcome such objections. They might advance a loan against a valuable object, for example, but then charge the loaner an increased sum to redeem the deposited article. In 1515, a German theologian named Johann Eck came up with a celebrated series of formulas that reclassified loans as investment contracts on which it was permissable openly to make a profit.

As Europe's merchants invested, they prompted technological innovations in fields such as metallurgy, shipbuilding, and printing. Groups of merchants combined to establish private banks and exchanges that financed technical developments or long voyages that might not realize a profit for a year or more. Success was not always guaranteed, however. Europe's constant wars made international investments particularly risky. Between 1587 and 1589, twenty large bankers went bankrupt in Spain and Italy. In the late sixteenth century, public banks emerged, that is, banks that were backed by government or municipal funds. Such institutions tended to take few risks, however, and rarely advanced money on speculative enterprises.

The Heyday of Antwerp

Europe's population began to rise after 1500—from around 61.6 million in 1500 to 78 million in 1600, according to some sources. The rise created both increased demand for food and goods and a larger, cheaper, workforce to produce them. It also fed the growth of cities and towns. Some were capitals and administrative centers for Europe's emerging nation-states. Others were ports such as Venice, Seville, Amsterdam, and Hamburg. Around 1550, Antwerp in Flanders was the continent's chief port, thanks in part to the Portuguese decision to use it for importing spices from India. The Antwerp bourse, or financial exchange, was the continent's leading money market.

At its height, Antwerp had some 90,000 inhabitants. When the Dutch revolted against their Spanish rulers in the Eighty Years' War in 1566, however, many citizens left Antwerp, which remained under Spanish control. The majority of the refugees headed north, where Amsterdam replaced Antwerp as Europe's financial heart. The Flemish immigrants brought to the Netherlands their craft skills, their capital for investment, and their expertise in the textiles industry. Others emigrated to France, Denmark, or Sweden, where they often rose to financial prominence, playing a part in the national economy. The physical movement of people—whether individuals, families, or whole communities—was an important way in which economic ideas and wealth spread throughout Europe.

The Role of Government

The growth of commercial activity in Europe owed much to the parallel emergence of more centralized forms of government. The new monarchs were the biggest spenders in Europe, because they had to pay for the bureaucracies and armies necessary to retain their power. They also adopted conspicuously expensive lifestyles to distinguish them from their subjects.

Centralized nation-states brought favorable conditions for trade. By increasing social discipline, they provided more protection from robbers on the roads, for example, and, eventually, a standardization of coinage and of internal tolls. By encouraging trade, monarchs and governments ensured that they would have sources of income in time of need. Governments adopted a system of public debt, which had been used in Italian city-states since the thirteenth century. The system used loans, rather than unpopular tax raises, to support the upkeep of armies, for example. Some firms, such as the Fuggers of Augsburg (*see 1:46*), amassed great fortunes by receiving trade concessions and properties in return for the supply of capital to Europe's royal families. By financing or

This gold florin was minted by the Medici family in Florence, Italy. Italian city-states each had their own system of coinage, complicating trade between them.

refusing to finance wars, such merchants now played an important role in the politics of Europe. Monarchs' reliance on merchants, meanwhile, saw them increasingly granting concessions that undermined the restrictive practices of the guilds.

The Tools of Trade

Increased trade brought an increased need for records and for easier ways to conduct business. An influential development came from the Italian Luca Pacioli (c. 1445–c. 1514), who developed "Italian accounting," the double-entry system of bookkeeping still widely used. The gradual introduction after the thirteenth century of

This portrait by an unknown artist shows Luca Pacioli, the inventor of modern accounting. The figure in the background is probably one of Pacioli's patrons, Duke Guidobalda of Urbino.

45

A Great Banking Dynasty

The emergence of large-scale business in the sixteenth century and the demand for capital investment saw the emergence of a number of fims that were in many ways the forerunners of the great financial institutions of today. Such companies were often ostensibly family concerns, such as the Grimaldi of Genoa in Italy. In reality, they drew together numerous investors to put capital into the firm in return for a fixed rate of interest. The great impetus behind their emergence was the constant need of western Europe's new monarchies for cash.

Of all the great banking families, the most successful and yet also the most representative were the Fuggers of Augsburg,

This portrait by Albrecht Dürer shows Jakob Fugger the Rich, the man who made the Fuggers Europe's preeminent merchant dynasty.

in Germany. Within two generations, the Fuggers established a firm which, in 1493, was able to finance the election of the Habsburg ruler Maximilian I as the Holy Roman emperor rather than the French candidate Francis I.

The Fuggers, like other so-called merchant princes of the day, made their money from trade. Hans Fugger, a weaver, moved to Augsburg in 1367. By virtue of advantageous marriages, he became a powerful figure in the town's weavers' guild and a member of the town council, as well as running a successful textile trade.

Hans Fuggers' two sons, Andreas and Jakob I, both trained as goldsmiths, meanwhile, but inherited the family company on their father's death in 1408. They dissolved their partnership in 1454. Andreas's branch of the family went on to amass great wealth, but it was ruined by unwise investments and a disastrous lawsuit near the end of the century.

Jakob was more cautious, having witnessed already the bankruptcy of his father-in-law, the master of a mint; he became a respected member of the merchants' guild. When Jakob died in 1469, two of his seven sons carried on his business. Ulrich and Georg expanded into international trade. Placing a brother in Rome to act as an agent, they took on the responsibility of sending back to the pope the money gained from the sale of church offices or indulgences. These paper certificates—said to give their buyers remittance from their sins—were an important source of church revenue.

At another branch of the company, meanwhile, in Venice, the youngest Fugger brother was learning his business. Jakob II had originally planned a career in the church but instead had turned to studying the modern forms of bookkeeping being developed by Luca Pacioli. Unhappily married and childless, the shrewd, sober Jakob dedicated himself to his work. He would become the greatest of the Fugger dynasty, earning himself the byname Jakob the Rich.

Moving to Switzerland, Jakob II lent money to Habsburg princes in return for shares in lucrative gold and silver mines in the Tirol. In Silesia, in modern Slovakia, he leased a copper mine in 1495 that he built into Europe's greatest mining center of that age. Over the course of time, the Fuggers had established a public company, inviting investments. Their capital was doubled when Jakob persuaded a prince-bishop to join as a silent partner. The new injection of cash funded Jakob's attempt to establish a monopoly over Europe's copper supply.

Jakob, who was by now the head of the whole firm, also engaged in any kind of commerce, including the spice trade with Asia. The early modern period was still an uncertain financial time: bankruptcies and devaluation were common. Jakob carefully divided the company's assets among cash, stock and merchandise, land and property, and precious stones. In 1507, as part of his acquisition of land, he bought two countships from Maximilian I, of whom he had long been the chief financial supporter; in 1514, the emperor made Fugger a count. The merchant had become a member of the nobility.

Fugger's loans to the Habsburg rulers brought him into conflict with some of his contemporaries. So, too, did his attempts to persuade the pope to modify the church's condemnation of charging interest on loans. The imperial authorities tried to challenge his monopolistic tendencies. Fugger was also the target of worker unrest both in his mines and in Augsburg. Among his severest critics were the German humanist thinker Ulrich von Hutten and the religious reformer Martin Luther, who criticized Fugger's support of the sale of indulgences. In his turn, Fugger viewed Luther's Protestant Reformation with alarm and stubbornly fought the new movement. For his old servants, meanwhile, Fugger built the Fuggerai, the world's oldest welfare settlement.

Jakob the Rich died in 1525 and left the company to his nephew Anton. Ambitious, talented, and a strict Roman Catholic, Anton made a decisive contribution toward the 1547 victory of the Holy Roman emperor Charles V in his wars against the Protestant Schmalkaldic League. As the company's mines became less profitable, Anton sought other avenues of business. With more or less success, he diversified into trading cloth to England, importing Hungarian cattle and spices, and trading slaves between Africa and America. By 1546, he had amassed the highest capital in the company's history, 5.1 million guilders. The constant demand for credit ate away at the Fuggers' reserves, however. After Anton's death in 1560, his son maintained the business on a more modest scale until it was finally dissolved in the middle of the seventeenth century.

Interest in the company had run out in the family. Jakob and Anton's descendants continued to live well, however, mainly thanks to their ancestors' prudent investments in land and titles. Unlike the strict merchant Jakob II, the later Fuggers lived according to their noble titles, attending Europe's universities to acquire the humanistic education that was considered essential for any member of the nobility. Three branches of the family still survive in modern Germany.

Still adorning the gateway to a family palace, the Fugger's family crest incorporates the double-headed eagle of the Austrian Habsburgs, to whom the merchant dynasty was closely affiliated.

Gold medallions and coins lie on a page of the secret journals of the Medici bank. The rise of trade and banking led to an increase in documentary records throughout Europe, making the period easier for historians to study than previous ages.

Arabic numerals—the digits 0 to 9 that we still use today—made computation simpler than the earlier unwieldy Roman numerals. The Arabic figure 48, for example, replaced the Roman numeral XXXXVIII.

Pacioli was among a number of gifted mathematicians who wrote practical manuals for merchants and traders. Such works provided advice on converting currencies that included different amounts of silver, calculating prices, and dividing profits between unequal investors. Banking concerns required employees with a high level of education to maintain the correspondence and accounting on which business depended. Many were classically educated in the new curriculum being encouraged by the humanist scholars of the Renaissance.

The largest single boon to international commerce drew on an old development, the bill of exchange, which replaced coins with paper bills. In 1543, an Antwerp financier remarked that "one can no more trade without bills of exchange than sail without water." The original bills were used as promises. A merchant in one city might sell a quantity of wool to another merchant and receive in exchange a bill of exchange promising him or his representa-

tive a quantity of timber in another city. The transaction could take place without the necessity of transporting bulky materials over long distances.

In the sixteenth century, bills of exchange became purely financial. They might be issued in one city to be repaid in another after a certain period, such as three months. In effect, such bills were loans that let merchants invest in numerous ventures without any goods changing hands at all.

A further commercial advance came in 1609 when the first Exchange Bank opened in Amsterdam. A public bank, it allowed people to make deposits, exchange currency, and later, take out loans. The bank both offered its depositors a safe home for their money—it had stores of gold and silver bullion to guarantee any credit it offered—and actively promoted industry and trade through investment.

Inflation

The growth of the European economy did not mean that it was stable. The periodic decision of the Spanish and French royal houses to cancel their debts ruined many private banks. In the sixteenth century, too, Europeans became conscious of a new phenomenon: inflation. Around 1500, prices began to rise quickly. Over the century, they rose an average of fourfold. As one historian has noted, the causes of inflation are clear enough to citizens of the twentieth century but were incomprehensible in the early modern age. From 1475 to 1620, Europeans found new sources of minerals in Bohemia and America, greatly increasing the number of coins in circulation. Industrial production and commerce did not match the increase in cash, so the money in circulation became worth less.

As a result, prices rose, slowly through the last decades of the fifteenth century but more rapidly by 1520. Wages rose, too, but not as fast and not as much. This imbalance produced a steady reduction in workers' real wages. In all of Europe, the living standards of the lower classes declined.

The lower classes often bore the negative side of Europe's trade boom. The loosening of the feudal bonds between peasants and landlords created a new class of workers who sold their labor or expertise for money. With these employed workers inevitably came an underclass of unemployed vagrants and beggars. Other workers' labor was only in seasonal demand. Accordingly, they lived on or near the breadline for much of the year. The wealth of Europe was by no means the wealth of all Europeans.

Scholasticism and the Universities

The Spread of Learning in Europe

Today, when everybody has to go to school in most of the Western world, it is difficult to imagine that this situation was not always true. About 1450, however, the mass of Europeans worked the land and never learned to read or write. Nor did many of their social betters. The only truly educated class was the clergy, although even some priests could not read. The word *clerk*, which now means an office worker who deals with accounts and written correspondence, derives from the word *cleric*, which meant a man who had studied theology and been ordained as a clergyman.

The minority of literate Europeans all wrote and spoke Latin, the language of the ancient Roman Empire. Although it was understood only by a relatively tiny elite, Latin crossed geographical and political boundaries and was one of the unifying

This sculpture of a cathedral scribe was carved during the fifteenth century in Mantua, in Italy. The spread of literacy owed much to the need of the Catholic Church for keeping reliable records of its property and income.

49

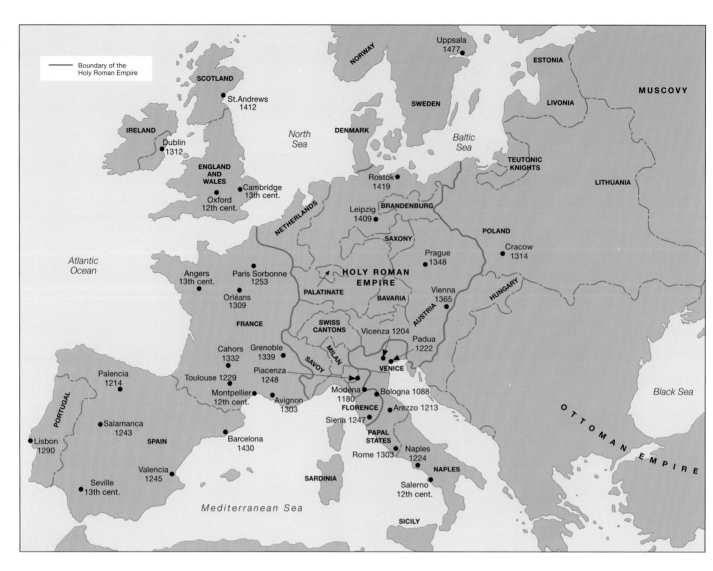

This map shows the location of some of Europe's major universities around 1450 and the dates of their founding. The Ottoman Empire is shown at its greatest extent in Europe, in about 1560.

bonds of Christendom. Latin was not Europe's only language, however. Ordinary people spoke what are called vernacular languages, the close ancestors of modern languages such as English, Italian, German, and French.

In the early modern period, parts of Europe were developing their own distinct vernaculars rather than using Latin. In the early fourteenth century, the Italian poet Dante Alighieri (1265–1321), known as Dante, wrote his long poem *The Divine Comedy* in Italian. In England, meanwhile, Geoffrey Chaucer (c. 1342–1400) wrote *The Canterbury Tales* in English. Such works lent respectability to vernacular, or native tongues. Regional languages tend to reinforce cultural barriers between people, however. As they came into greater prominence, vernaculars acted as corrosive agents that helped to undermine the unity of Christendom.

Formal Education

Despite the increasing use of the vernacular, Latin remained the language of formal education. During most of the Middle

Ages, the education of the clergy took place mainly in monasteries, although some enlightened rulers founded schools at their palace courts. The most illustrious of those royal schools was founded by Charlemagne at Aachen in the eighth century.

Early in the thirteenth century, two new orders of friars—the Franciscans and the Dominicans—emerged to reinforce Christian doctrine. The friars traveled widely, teaching all over Europe, though their teachings were focused on religion.

As part of Europe's general revival in the twelfth century, universities emerged in many urban centers, particularly in Italy, France, and England. The friars were drawn to these new seats of learning, especially Paris, where they established schools for members of their orders. Talented friar-scholars soon entered the universities to study for a degree in theology.

The First Universities

The first university in Europe was founded at Bologna, in Italy, in 1088. Where a university was founded was often largely a matter of chance. Princes seldom founded

Such quarrels hinged on the interpretation of law, which was often decided by appealing to old legal decisions or by taking arguments from ancient authorities, known as the church fathers. Such procedures created a demand for men trained in the law. A similar situation exists today in the United States, where some lawyers try to settle arguments by referring to the intentions of the Founders who drew up the American Constitution in 1787.

Student Life

Students, who were all male, began university at about the age of fourteen or fifteen. Most of them lodged in private houses or

This detail from a nineteenth-century French illustration shows the early scholar Peter Abelard. Abelard's reputation as a theologian drew many students to what became the University of Paris.

universities in their capitals; nor did universities necessarily arise in religious centers such as cathedral cities. They were communities of young men interested in learning and more often than not drawn to a particular place simply because an individual teacher of repute was there.

Bologna developed around Irnerius, a teacher of Roman law. Paris owed more to the teacher Peter Abelard (1079–c. 1144) than to the cathedral school of Notre Dame, which was its headquarters. Students flocked to Oxford in England to learn from Vacarius, another expert on the Roman law laid down in the Code of Justinian in the sixth century. By 1450, more than sixty universities stretched from Coimbra in Portugal to Prague in Bohemia.

One reason for the proliferation of universities was that, as royal government grew, monarchs needed administrators. Another reason was the revival of trade and the growth of companies and banking houses that needed staff. A further stimulus to the growth of education lay in the struggle for dominance between the pope and Europe's secular rulers, which led to quarrels over the rights and privileges of each.

This undated illustration shows students at a university in the late Middle Ages. While the students follow the lesson, officials called proctors patrol to keep order.

hospices run by townspeople. Scholars proved volatile, however, and were prone to riot to display their displeasure with various aspects of life. By the end of the thirteenth century, most universities had built halls of residence where they could keep their students under close supervision. At Oxford and Cambridge in England, residence in halls was compulsory.

Students' rooms were cold, seldom provided with fires, and often had wooden shutters in the windows rather than glass. Students were required to dress as nearly alike as possible when they took their two daily meals together. All sorts of contemporary pleasures were outlawed: keeping ferrets, hawks, or hunting dogs; playing musical instruments or singing; playing dice, chess, and other "dishonest games." Students had a curfew of 8:00 P.M. in winter or 9:00 P.M. in summer. Offenders against the rules had to pay fines.

It took a long time to qualify for a degree. A course in the liberal arts led to a first degree, the Bachelor of Arts, after four or five years' study. The final examinations had no written papers. Students had to answer questions on the spot put to them by their tutors.

The arts course had two parts. The trivium included rhetoric, logic and philosophy, and natural philosophy, or science. The quadrivium comprised math, geometry, astronomy, and music. The trivium was by far the more important of the two parts, teaching all the subjects it covered from a Christian viewpoint with reference to the Bible and the works of the church fathers. A student who passed his first examinations was required to teach for two years before proceeding to three more years' study for an M.A. (Master of Arts).

International Community

Europe's universities formed an international community. Since all university instruction and all scholarship were carried on in Latin, people from all over Christendom could communicate. Scholars traveled freely from one university to another.

Freedom of thought was less easy, however. Church authorities oversaw all teaching and had powers to punish teachers who strayed out of line. In general, the clergy and many scholars saw the function of the universities as not so much to discover new things about the world as to transmit established truths to the next generation. These established truths were the orthodox doctrines of the Catholic Church. Students were largely expected to absorb existing knowledge, not to question it.

The Arab Contribution

Much scholarly effort was directed at incorporating into western Europe's received body of truth ancient Greek and Roman sources that were just becoming known in the West. Many sources were carried to Europe by Greek scholars from Constantinople after the capital of the Byzantine empire fell to the Muslims in 1453. The works included some that formed the basis of much Western thought for centuries. They included the technology of Hero of Alexandria, the mathematics of Euclid and Archimedes, the medicine of Hippocrates and Galen, and the Roman law encased in the Code of Justinian.

Many of the classical sources that made their way to Europe owed their survival to Arab scholars. When the Arabs conquered what is now known as the Middle East, they had inherited western knowledge preserved there since the days of ancient Greece. Translators turned out Arabic ver-

Drawn in the fifteenth century, this manuscript illustration shows a lecturer at the University of Bologna, Italy. Such a lecturer was responsible for passing on orthodox teaching to his pupils, not encouraging them to think independently.

sions of Greek texts and inspired Europeans to make the same exploration of "the Greek sciences." The tradition of scholarship in the Arab world kept alive knowledge that had vanished from Europe during the so-called Dark Ages.

Sicily and Spain

The Byzantine Empire was not the only place where European and Arab culture met. On the Mediterranean island of Sicily, rulers such as Roger II (1095–1154) and Frederick II (1194–1250) had presided over courts that reflected influences from the Arabs who had conquered the island in the tenth century.

Under Roger, Sicily was the only place in Europe where scholars could study Greek and Arabic, then the most important scientific language. At the same time, the crusades against the Muslims were isolating western from eastern culture elsewhere in Europe. Frederick II, who was also Holy Roman emperor, encouraged the interchange of scholarly ideas at his court, which combined Latin, German, Jewish, Greek, and Arab influences. He was known as the *stupor mundi*, the "wonder of the world." Sicily's role as a cultural melting pot ended after the island was reclaimed by the papacy in the late thirteenth century.

In Spain, meanwhile, much of the peninsula had come under the rule of the Moors of North Africa. Muslim and Christian scholars explored eastern, Greek, and Latin sources in the libraries of Seville, Granada, and Córdoba. Muslim Spain influenced scholarship in neighboring France, thus helping to stimulate the development of humanist thought in the rest of Europe.

Cardinal Bessarion

One of the most famous of the Greek scholars who fled Constantinople in 1453 was Cardinal Bessarion (1403–1472). A theologian, humanist, and book collector, Bessarion moved to Italy, where he donated his great library to the Republic of Venice.

Bessarion's ambition was to translate into Latin Ptolemy's *Almagest*. The work, which was available only in Greek, detailed Ptolemy's view of the universe as a series of concentric spheres with Earth at the center. When Bessarion died, the work was completed by his colleagues. The book provided a vital spur to scientific investigation of the universe, even though it was proved wrong by the discoveries made in the sixteenth century of how heavenly bodies actually behaved.

The physical sciences were not highly regarded in a world where logic and theol-

King Edward's Tower rises above Trinity College at Cambridge, England, founded in 1546. The tower is named for Edward VI, who ruled from 1547 to 1553. Universities supplied many of the bureaucrats royalty required to administer its kingdoms and taxes.

A doorway of the Bodleian Library in Oxford still preserves the Latin inscription that identifies it as the entrance to the school of grammar and history.

53

Education Outside the Universities

This detail from a wood panel painted around 1440 commemorates Pope Innocent III's recognition of the Franciscan order in 1209. The monastic order became a major provider of education in Europe in the early modern world.

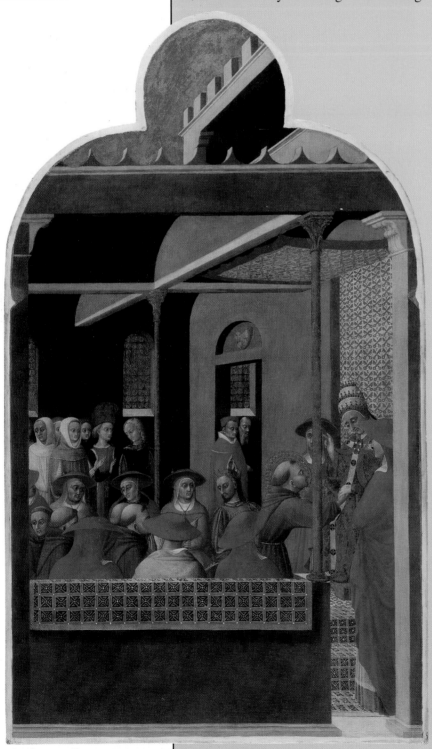

Europe's universities taught only a tiny fraction of all Europeans. Indeed, the number of scholars was so small that the universities are sometimes condemned as being obscurantist, meaning that they treated knowledge as the preserve of an elite and denied it to the general public.

For most Europeans, any form of education remained rare in the middle of the fifteenth century. Reading and writing were rare. With the growth of trade after the twelfth century, however, and the proliferation of correspondence and accounts, it was becoming advantageous, particularly in towns, to be able to read.

Education in Europe was traditionally provided by monastic orders. From about the twelfth century, however, monastic schools closed classes to all but those who wished to become monks. At about the same time, however, the Catholic Church made education in grammar a duty for all cathedrals. Cathedrals established schools where future clerics studied Latin and theology but could also study practical subjects such as wool processing, navigation, agriculture, and medicine.

As universities emerged, these urban schools formed the basis of a general growth in education. Even nonclerics could attend grammar schools, so called for the emphasis they placed on the study of classical languages. New schools were organized by groups such as merchant and trades guilds. Religious fraternities, such as the Brethren of the Common Life in the Netherlands, also established schools; their pupils included the outstanding humanist Erasmus.

Despite such efforts, grammar schools remained scarce. England had only about forty by 1400. Other sources of education were available, however. Students might attend schools for writing or for singing. Parish priests provided informal schooling in the Christian faith. People similarly passed on the practical math needed in everyday life. After printed books became common in the mid–fifteenth century, literacy began to grow rapidly.

Girls had far less chance than boys to receive a formal education. Rich families sometimes provided tutors for girls, but their education focused on household management, playing music, and similar activities. It was not until the sixteenth century that female orders, such as the Ursulines, began to provide elementary education for girls.

Among those who also often missed out on the growth in education were the sons of the nobility. They still followed a feudal education that taught them knightly concepts of courtesy and duty. Rather than attend school and university, boys acted as pages and squires in noble homes and castles. Such an education, suited to a disappearing society, left the nobility unprepared to face the modern world.

Popular education received a number of boosts in the early sixteenth century. Humanists such as the Spaniard Juan Luis Vives emphasized the importance of popular education. Vives argued that city authorities and craft guilds had a duty to provide schools and recommended that students should visit workshops to learn practical skills. Vives also suggested that women should be educated, though in different subjects because of the different lives they would lead.

The largest boost to education, however, came from the Protestant Reformation in Germany. The religious reformer Martin Luther saw reading the Bible as essential to increasing personal faith. He wanted to open schools that would be free to boys and girls from all classes and financed by public funds. All children should study, if only for a few hours when they were not working in the field. Luther's theory directly associated spiritual salvation with the ability to read. From around 1550, German princes began to organize new schools along the lines suggested by Luther. As the Reformation spread, so too did similar schools. The link between education and religion remained as strong as ever.

A manuscript illumination from around 1300 shows students receiving education in a German monastery. At bottom right, students share a scarce manuscript text.

A group of tourists visit the preserved anatomical theater at the University of Bologna. The early universities provided scholars' first opportunity to perform dissection, enabling them to test wisdom handed down by earlier Greek and Arab scholars.

ogy dominated intellectual activity. The ground was laid for some later advances in science, however. At Paris, Jean Buridan demonstrated the inadequacy of Aristotle's laws of motion and attempted to establish his own law of impetus. His methods—observation and experiment—were those that future scientists would follow.

Meanwhile, knowledge of anatomy was increased by dissecting human bodies. Herbs were collected for remedies, coastlines plotted with compasses and astrolabes, and math principles used to design domes and arches. Some studies are now discredited, such as astrology, which gauged the stars' and planets' influence on human behavior, and alchemy, which sought to change one metal into another.

In the Service of Religion

The study of religion, or theology, remained the focus of education. Since Europeans believed that life had meaning only as it was lived in fulfilment of God's purposes, the thinkers of the age saw the object of intellectual inquiry as explaining and interpreting God's will. This purpose created a great difficulty. One of the basic beliefs of the Catholic Church was that

God was mysterious and that His eternal purposes were beyond the understanding of mortals. Medieval thinkers devised ever more subtle arguments to overcome the dilemma this presented.

There was also a practical reason why most people studied the same subject. Before printing, when every book had to be copied by hand, universities did not have large libraries. In the absence of a range of books, group discussion played a large part in learning. A good memory, a quick intelligence in debate, and the ability to construct arguments skillfully on the spot were essential qualities for success.

When instruction did rely on the written word, universities provided numerous copies of only one or two books. All students studied the same book and demonstrated that they had digested its contents. The Bible was one such volume; the writings of the most famous church father, Saint Augustine of Hippo (354–430), filled another. The most widely used textbook, however, was written by Peter Lombard (c. 1095–1160). Educated at Bologna and Reims, Lombard taught at the cathedral school that became the University of Paris. Published in the mid–twelfth century, *Four*

Books of the Sentences contained selections from the church fathers and medieval scholars. It shaped the content of theological studies for the next two centuries.

Schoolmen and Scholasticism

The scholars who taught the orthodox doctrines of the Christian Church were known as Schoolmen, and the system that they taught was called Scholasticism. Scholasticism developed, in large part, as the Church's answer to an unsettling challenge from ancient Greece, which came in the writings of the greatest of classical Greek thinkers, Aristotle (384–322 B.C.E.).

Aristotle lived long before the founding of Christianity, when no one believed that there was only one God who created and ruled over the whole universe. The myths of the Greeks and the Romans tell of many gods and goddesses. Although Aristotle wrote on almost every aspect of human thought, therefore, including politics and science, he did so with no reference to a supreme supernatural being. Aristotle stressed the importance of empirical observation and of human reason, or logic, in understanding the world. This approach was at variance with the implicit faith on which Christian theology depended.

Thomas Aquinas

Christian scholars could not ignore Aristotle's work. The rediscovery of his texts made him widely known and respected in Europe and the Islamic world as a philosopher and scholar. Now the Schoolmen devoted their energies to combating the fact that such a great thinker could interpret the world in a way that made no reference to God. The greatest scholar to do this was Thomas Aquinas (1225–1274), from Naples, who was made a saint in 1323. His greatest work, the *Summa Theologiae*, aimed to summarize the complete Christian view of the world. Aquinas began the work in 1266; it was still unfinished when he died.

Aquinas agreed with some of Aristotle's opinions, such as the fact that all ideas originated in the senses. Aquinas tried to reconcile that opinion with the view that whatever proceeded from reason was compatible with faith in an all-knowing God. Aquinas argued in favor of the correlation of sense, knowledge, reason, and faith.

Questioning Scholasticism

As Schoolmen after Aquinas wrestled with the apparent contradiction between reason and faith, their arguments grew so abstract as to have little connection with anything that ordinary people could understand. Schoolmen were said to have heated debates about subjects such as how many angels could dance on the head of a pin. Eventually, the obscurity of Scholasticism provoked a reaction in the direction of freer, less constrained thought. That reaction went by the name of humanism, whose chief luminary was the Dutchman Desiderius Erasmus (c. 1466–1536).

In this contemporary woodcut, Saint Thomas Aquinas lectures to a group including the twelfth-century Islamic scholar Ibn Rushd, known in the West as Averroës. Ibn Rushd was one of the most prominent scholars who tried to reconcile Islamic and Greek ideas.

Erasmus went to the University of Paris in 1495 but was disappointed by the theology he found there: obscure arguments and a preoccupation with formal detail and empty propositions. "Those studies," he complained, "can make a man opinionated and contentious; can they make him wise?"

To Erasmus, the Schoolmen seemed remote from true religion and daily life. In his popular book *The Praise of Folly*, he wrote that it would be prudent "to pass over the theologians in silence." Erasmus observed that formalism withered the Schoolmen's lives. If someone's thinking were no more than an arrangement of traditional arguments, then his or her life was nothing more than an arrangement of traditional habits and observances. The humanists would loosen the thinking that Scholasticism had hardened.

The Importance of Universities

By the fifteenth century, most students attended university in order to qualify for careers at court or in the service of landowners with large estates. Theology remained the focus of education, but the range of subjects available also included Latin grammar, logic, medicine, anatomy, astronomy, musical theory, and elementary science, called natural philosophy.

The debates of the Schoolmen earned universities a reputation for obscurantism, or keeping knowledge from the public and making it the preserve only of the elite. Nevertheless, the universities as institutions played a vital role in stimulating thought. They gave scholars virtual independence to develop various studies, such as anatomy through dissection, largely without answering directly to the church or a temporal ruler, as earlier scholars had.

Early universities taught professional subjects, such as law, theology, and medicine. By producing trained graduates, the universities were instrumental in the administrative development of Europe's nation-states. Western thought remains to a large extent shaped by the canon of classical authors and works established by the university curricula. Europe's other contemporary tradition of learning, however, concerning humanism and the arts, developed outside the university curriculum.

Perhaps most important, universities provided a means by which Europeans became more conscious of the age in which they lived. Beyond the arguments of the Schoolmen, scholars studied classical languages not as a dry academic exercise but as a way to better understand history. By appreciating the past, they could better understand their own time. It was in this consciousness of their position in relation to what had gone before that the scholars of the fifteenth century began to see themselves as belonging to a new world: the modern world.

Humanism and the Spread of Knowledge

The Emergence of a New View of the World

Universities began to emerge throughout Europe from the twelfth century (*see 1:50*). Learning remained the privilege of a tiny elite, however. Most people received no education in reading and writing. They learned the skills they needed for everyday life: how to plow or mend a fence, for instance, or how to make shoes and clothing. For information about other matters, they depended largely on what the priest told them at church. This often amounted to a few elementary religious ideas that were presented as unquestioned truths.

The Limited Spread of Knowledge
A number of factors limited the spread of knowledge. Church and government affairs were conducted in Latin, not in the vernac-

This modern reconstruction shows the press invented by Johannes Gutenberg for printing with movable type. In the foreground are early examples of printed works.

This modern facsimile shows a Latin text on an illuminated parchment, surrounded by the tools necessary for the laborious task of creating decorated manuscripts.

Gutenberg and Printing

In about 1450 came one of the shaping moments of Western civilization, the invention of the printing press. In many ways, this was not an invention at all. The techniques of printing had actually been known in China for some 600 years but had never been transmitted to the West, where they were independently discovered later. Several people were developing the process at the same time but credit for the most important technological advance usually goes to the German Johannes Gutenberg (c. 1390–1468).

Gutenberg's breakthrough involved printing on paper with movable type. This was vastly cheaper and more versatile than the earlier block printing. In block printing, a craftsman carved a whole page on a block of wood, which was then inked and stamped onto the printing surface. Each block took a lot of labor to produce and soon wore out. Movable type combined individual metal letters to form words and then reused them on another page. Gutenberg employed an alloy of lead, tin, and antimony to cast durable letters that could be used over and over again.

Gutenberg also invented a new, more lasting kind of ink, based on that used in oil paints, with which to coat his letters. He also made adaptations to machines, called presses, which were commonly used for making wine and paper. With these modified machines he was able to "press," or print, the ink that coated his metal letters onto handmade paper. For clients who could afford it, Gutenberg's process also allowed him to print on vellum.

Among the first books Gutenberg printed with this new process were a Latin grammar, an encyclopedia, and a magnificent Latin Bible, usually called the Gutenberg Bible. The book is also sometimes called the Mainz Bible, for the wealthy trading town of Mainz, on the Rhine River, where Gutenberg set up his press. Forty-seven copies of the Bible still survive.

Luxury Items

Despite Gutenberg's invention, books initially were rare and expensive. Printers produced no more than 200 copies of each work, which were usually sold as loose pages and bound for specific customers. The final volume was itself often a work of art. Covers were made of a precious fabric such as velvet, silk, or leather and often had elaborate metal clasps to keep the book closed. Pages were decorated with gold leaf and hand-painted pictures called illuminations. Gutenberg used many of the

ular languages spoken by ordinary people. Lawyers and priests learned Latin and thus became the principal people with access to academic knowledge.

Until the middle of the fifteenth century, all texts had to be laboriously written down by hand. The scribes used quill pens made of goose feathers and usually wrote on fine calf or sheepskin called vellum. People did know how to make paper, however. In the fifteenth century, the Italian town of Fabriano was a center of the paper industry. Every single copy of any piece of writing—whether a poem, a government document, or a whole Bible—had to be made separately by royal clerks or monks. This work was time-consuming and expensive. Only the wealthiest could afford books.

Even the inks were difficult to handle. Two kinds of ink were in common use from the thirteenth century onward. One of them was prepared by mixing iron salt and oak gall, a sticky substance produced by insects on the bark of oak trees. The other was made by mixing soot with gum and water. It had to be constantly stirred to prevent it from hardening in its pot.

This portrait shows Johannes Gutenberg, who is commonly credited with inventing Europe's first printing press. Gutenberg later lost all rights to his invention in a dispute with a business partner.

decorating techniques associated with manuscripts. Thus, inevitably, his books were expensive and slow to produce. He did, however, attract clients who, though not necessarily scholars themselves, wished to amass libraries that reflected their wealth, status, and culture. Nobles such as the princes of Italian city-states collected valuable works and employed scholars to study them. With the coming of the luxury book, some historians suggest, knowledge became like any other commodity that could be bought and sold.

The Spread and Impact of Books

Before long, printed books became much more common. By 1500, there were as many as nine million books in Europe, produced by printers established in leading cities, such as Rome, Paris, and Cologne. In Venice in 1501, Aldus Manutius published the first small, portable, relatively cheap books. More people wanted to own books now, and Manutius printed 1,000 copies at a time. Manutius's books can be seen as precursors of popular paperbacks, although they were intended primarily for scholars of Greek and Latin.

Printed books contributed greatly to a general process of change that was taking place in European ideas and literature. Books made it possible to spread new ideas faster and to a wider audience. There was a thriving market not just for legitimate editions of the latest scholarly works—some complete with diagrams—but also for pirated editions issued by unscrupulous printers.

Books and Languages

Although the earliest books were in Latin, books soon appeared in the vernacular languages spoken by ordinary people. This development had two apparently contradictory effects. On the one hand, it contributed to a fragmentation of the previously unified world of learning; on the other, it brought a new unity to the vernacular languages.

In most countries, there was no standard language. Regional accents and dialects were much more pronounced than they are

This page from the Gutenberg Bible, printed in 1455, shows the opening of the Gospel According to Saint Luke. The decoration shows how Gutenberg employed the techniques of manuscript illumination to enhance the printed text.

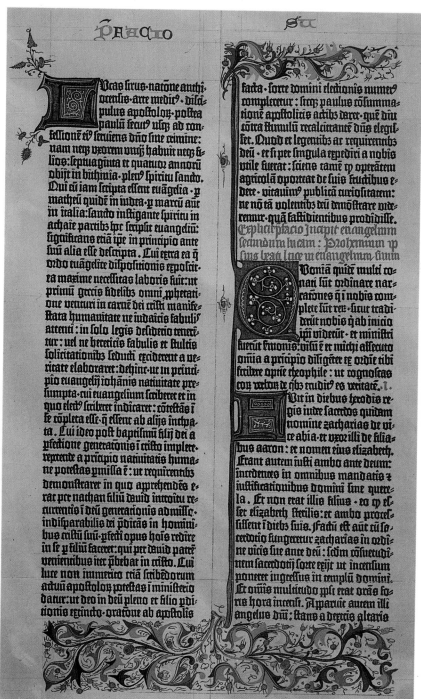

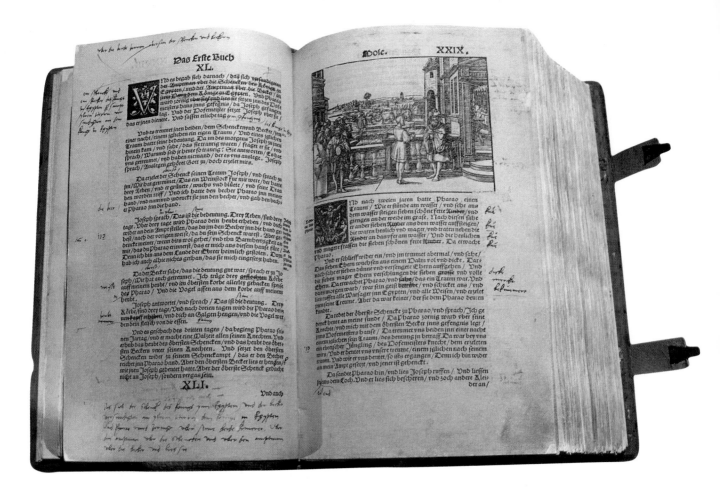

This pre-1541 edition of Martin Luther's German Bible features notes made by Luther himself. Like other early books, this volume has metal clasps to hold it shut when it is not in use.

today. Even those people who could write in the vernacular simply spelled words as they thought they might sound. Printed books brought an increasing standardization of spelling and grammar, beginning a trend toward the breakdown of regional varieties of languages. Over the centuries, the English came to speak the language standard in London, the French the language standard in Paris.

For the first time, people who learned to read gained access to knowledge that had been inaccessible when everything was in Latin. Of the many books published in vernaculars, the most important and influential was the Bible, which appeared in large numbers by the beginning of the sixteenth century. There had been vernacular translations of the Bible before, but few copies were in circulation. Now, more people could actually read the Bible, instead of relying on priests to tell them what it said.

The opportunity to read the Bible for oneself was to have profound significance during the Protestant Reformation (*see 2:151*). Martin Luther, who himself translated the Bible into German, based the Protestant faith on close, personal study of the word of God. Protestant reformers also exploited the printing press to produce pamphlets about their ideas and win popular support. Religious authorities were already aware of the power of the printed word. Mainz, where European printing began, also saw the first recorded suppression of books in 1486, when the city established Europe's first censorship office.

The Rise of Humanism

The earliest books ranged from new scholarly works to editions of ancient Greek and Roman authors. The popularity of these classical works both reflected and encouraged a new intellectual climate. Printing fed a growing appetite for classical texts. In the independent city-states of Italy, in particular, citizens sought a social and moral framework that encompassed their lives more fully than traditional feudal or ecclesiastical values. For parallels with their own society, they turned to the study of ancient Rome and, thus, to ancient Greece, to which Roman thought owed a great debt.

A new type of scholar emerged, whose purpose was to make classical literature intelligible to patrons who were often wealthy merchants, bankers, or princes. Such scholars were known as humanists, from the Latin phrase *studia humanitatis*. The name, still reflected in the word *humanities*, represented a comprehensive intellectual discipline, based on the study of classical texts, that incorporated grammar, rhetoric, history, poetry, and moral philosophy. The humanists believed that such studies could provide a basis for civil and political fulfillment.

Humanist studies led many fifteenth-century Italians to become absorbed in the past for its own sake. They believed that Europe was emerging from a period of cultural impoverishment and saw themselves as different from both their European contemporaries and their Italian forebears. The perceived difference was one reason for the optimism and confidence of Renaissance Italy. Many Italians retained, however, the belief that the classical world was superior in all ways to their own.

Recovering the Classics

The first task of the humanists was to recover classical texts. Europeans had remained familiar with classical literature throughout the Middle Ages but had concentrated on practical works that increased their store of facts, such as the medical studies of Galen and the logical method of Aristotle. The humanists sought also to study ancient poetry and philosophy, which had long been neglected.

Encouraged and often funded by their patrons, scholars became single-minded in their pursuit of manuscripts. Nicolao Nicoli, for example, sold all his farms to buy books. A contemporary recorded Nicoli's discovery of a lost work by the first-century B.C.E. Roman author Cicero: "The book was found in a chest in a very old church; this chest had not been opened

for a long time and they found the book, a very ancient example, while searching for evidence containing certain ancient rights."

Humanists copied and edited classical works for their patrons and developed techniques of textual criticism in order to establish works' authenticity. By the time printing was invented, most Roman texts had been recovered. Printing was particularly important, therefore, in disseminating Greek literature. The first Greek lexicon appeared in 1478, the first grammar in 1497. The Venetian Aldus Manutius specialized in producing Greek texts.

The artist Andrea del Castagno painted this portrait of Petrarch in the fifteenth century. Dubbed the father of humanism, the fourteenth-century Petrarch was a dominant figure in European thought.

This handwritten and illuminated copy of one of Petrarch's poems was created in Bologna, Italy, in 1414.

Greek studies reflected humanism's international culture. The movement owed an enormous debt to Greek scholars of the Byzantine world, who had preserved most of the classical texts that inspired the movement. Through their conquests in the eastern Mediterranean, Muslim peoples had acquired Greek culture and preserved the traditions of scholarship at a time when Europe was undergoing economic and cultural stagnation. This heritage was later passed to Europe, either by trading contacts between Italian city-states and the Islamic world or from the Islamic universities of Asia Minor and Moorish Spain. When Byzantine scholars, including Cardinal Bessarion (*see 1:53*), stayed in Italy after a 1438 council between the Catholic and Orthodox churches, their students retrieved manuscripts from the Byzantine capital, Constantinople, until it was captured by the Ottoman Turks in 1453.

Petrarch

Humanism did not start suddenly in the fifteenth century. The fourteenth-century Italian scholar and poet, Francesco Petrarca (1304–1374), known as Petrarch, is often called the father of humanism. Petrarch was a new kind of intellectual. He made his living from writing and by acting as a consultant to rich and powerful patrons. His interests ranged widely. He was a lawyer and cleric who also wrote love poetry. Above all, he was devoted to the writers of

The church of San Biagio stands beneath the hill town of Montepulciano in Tuscany, Italy. The church's domed design reflects humanist architectural ideas that placed worshipers at the heart of religious services.

ancient Greece and Rome, tracking down and publicizing forgotten manuscripts. Petrarch was eager to make his way in the world. He liked mixing with powerful people and was skilled at self-promotion.

The Variety of Humanism

Humanism remained rooted in a devotion to classical learning, but its scholars varied widely in their interests. Some studied only textual matters. Others were so convinced that Latin was the only language of literary merit that they condemned Petrarch for writing in Italian. Other humanists, skilled in rhetoric, or the rules of composition, acted as secretaries to princes and councils, preparing public documents or speeches linking contemporary politics to classical antiquity. When republican Florence was resisting an aristocratic takeover, humanists encouraged resistance by drawing parallels with republican Rome.

Members of the Platonic Academy in Florence, meantime, rejected what they saw as the narrow scholasticism associated with Aristotle (*see 1:57*) in favor of the teachings of the fourth-century B.C.E. philosopher Plato. The humanists adapted to Christian thought Plato's teaching that all truth and beauty in the world are pale reflections of the supreme truth and beauty that exist eternally in the mind of God. People should try to understand these universal forms through reason, although their understanding could only ever be imper-

fect. Italians such as the Florentine religious leader Savonarola condemned the Neo-Platonists for heresy.

The Influence of Humanism

The spirit of humanism was felt in a wide range of activities. Mapmaking boomed. At about the same time as Christopher Columbus was planning his voyage across the Atlantic Ocean, the Italian Paolo Toscanelli was writing books to prove that such a voyage would be successful. Columbus himself was inspired to make his journey in 1492 by the Greek scholar Ptolemy's *Geography*, a second-century work that had recently been printed.

Humanism had a profound effect on religious worship. Medieval cathedrals all reflected the same basic plan. They were long, with a central aisle, or nave, that led the eye toward an altar at its eastern end. Soaring columns and high-pitched roofs led the eye upward. The very shape of the building encouraged worshipers to lift their

thoughts upward to heaven or toward the distant altar and its crucifix.

Inspired by classical examples from ancient Rome, humanist architects built churches that were not elongated but focused on a central point. They placed the altar in the center of the church, beneath a dome. To appreciate the building, worshipers had to look around in all directions. In this way, architects placed the congregation at the center of worship, reflecting humanity's pivotal place in the world.

Machiavelli and Politics

An important expression of one humanist interpretation of the world came in a book called *The Prince*. Written by the Italian Niccolò Machiavelli (1469–1527) in 1513, *The Prince* explained to rulers how best to stay in power. The duty of every ruler was to gain power and hold on to it by whatever means. Machiavelli said that rulers should instil fear in their subjects to command obedience. The word *Machiavellian* soon came to be used to describe an unprincipled schemer.

The Prince displeased many people because it paid no attention to the accepted idea that rulers were God's agents on earth and should behave in ways that would be judged favorably by God. Machiavelli left God out of his account. "I have thought it proper," he wrote, "to represent things as they are in life, rather than as they are imagined." Machiavelli's secular and deeply cynical view of the world was profoundly influential. It represented only one strand of humanist thinking, however. Humanism as a whole supported a rich and varied approach to the world.

The International Links of Humanism

Humanism was largely developed by laypeople, independently of either religious orders and institutions or the universities. As the movement spread through Europe, humanists across the continent formed their own scholarly community, corresponding and visiting one another to debate their ideas and expand their knowledge. Desiderius Erasmus (c. 1466–1536), one of the greatest humanists, turned down an offer of citizenship from the city of Zurich, in Switzerland, saying that he preferred to remain a citizen of the world.

Erasmus, who was born in Holland, was a major figure in Europe's intellectual life. He was closely associated with trying to revive simple Christian piety in opposition to the wealth and corruption within the Roman Catholic Church. Erasmus was also keenly interested in politics and so became

This classical-style statue from the eighteenth century shows the Italian Niccolò Machiavelli. Machiavelli is known for his argument that rulers use any means possible to attain power. 65

Humanism and Change

For many historians, the emergence of humanism was a critical element in the transition from the medieval to the modern world. Not only did it encourage a view of the world centered on humanity rather than God, it also revived the tradition of classical scholarship. In accumulating, translating, and studying the works of the ancient Greeks and Romans, the humanists created the core of works that underlay Western thought for at least three centuries.

The humanists looked back rather than forward. They were more concerned with re-creating the glories of a vanished golden age than with surpassing them. In the process, however, scholars sometimes improved on classical models. Their refinements of the intellectual heritage made humanism a force for change that helped to usher in the modern era.

Such a role was not inevitable, however. In other cultures, intellectual activity acted to reinforce tradition rather than encourage change. Scholars of the Talmud, for example, the body of Jewish theological knowledge, pursued narrow analysis of the great works of the Jewish faith and the cabala, a doctrine that included elements of mystery and magic. Lacking a state, Jewish scholars were not interested in political or social structures, as their Christian counterparts were.

In the Islamic world, meanwhile, Muslim scholars had from the eighth to the twelfth centuries made great advances in math, medicine, astronomy, and chemistry. Contact with such advances helped revive European scholarship. At the same time, however, Islamic scholarship declined. Politics in the Islamic world promoted the consolidation of tradition over innovation. Muslim states were theocracies, meaning that they were run as instruments of religion dedicated to the protection of Islam. The privileged elite of scholars was tied to maintaining both the state and the Islamic faith.

Chinese scholars, meanwhile, worked in a tradition of Confucianism, a belief system that discouraged activities such as competition or trade, both of which were important engines of change in Europe. Almost as soon as gunpowder was introduced to Europe, for example, engineers saw its potential for making weapons to use in the warfare endemic on the continent. The Chinese, meanwhile, had learned how to make gunpowder 400 years earlier but had not developed gunpowder weapons. They reserved gunpowder mainly for fireworks.

Chinese scholars were concerned with cataloging the world rather than changing it. They compiled the *Yung-lo ta-tien*, an encyclopedia whose creation took 2,000 scholars five years. Completed in 1409, it comprised more than 11,000 volumes. They were too expensive to print, so only three handwritten copies were produced.

The very ambition of such imperial-sponsored projects undermined any contribution they might have made to a process of modernization. In contrast, the European universities gave individual scholars the circumstances to pursue their own studies independent of any royal or religious interference.

This 1520 print shows the trademark of Jodocus Ascensius, a printer in Paris, France. The proliferation of books encouraged independent scholarship in Europe, making scholarly texts more easily available than anywhere else in the world.

This contemporary woodcarving from Germany shows Erasmus in the guise of a wandering pilgrim.

the friend of Sir Thomas More at the court of King Henry VIII of England.

More (1478–1535), who became lord chancellor of England, exhibited a characteristic humanist blend of old and new. He followed the medieval practice of wearing a hair shirt, a rough garment that irritated the skin, worn by Christians as a penance and a constant reminder that they were born into sin. More was also an author, a trained lawyer, and a brilliant thinker who delighted in the new learning of his age.

Political Satires

Humanist scholars were welcome at royal courts, where princes sought their advice or enjoyed the enhanced reputation scholars brought to their court. Close acquaintance with government led humanists to speculate on politics and social organization. Machiavelli, who served in the government of Florence from 1498 to 1512, wrote *The Prince* in an attempt to gain favor with Lorenzo de' Medici, who overthrew that government in 1513. Erasmus and More also wrote about politics, but they adopted a style that used satire to expose corruption in both church and state.

The very title of Erasmus's *The Praise of Folly*, written in 1509, declares its intentions. The book offers a biting attack on bad government, as well as religious hypocrisy and vanity generally. More's *Utopia*, published in 1516, speculates on an imaginary place where society is governed by principles of religious tolerance and social cooperation in contrast to the societies of selfishness and greed More perceived in Christian Europe at the time.

Both *The Praise of Folly* and *Utopia* reveal a deep concern for the lives of ordinary people and respect for the social and

67

This ceramic plate bears the coat of arms of the Medici family. In its patronage of the arts, its extensive banking interests, and its grip on political power in Florence, the family symbolized Machiavelli's ideal of the virtuous citizen.

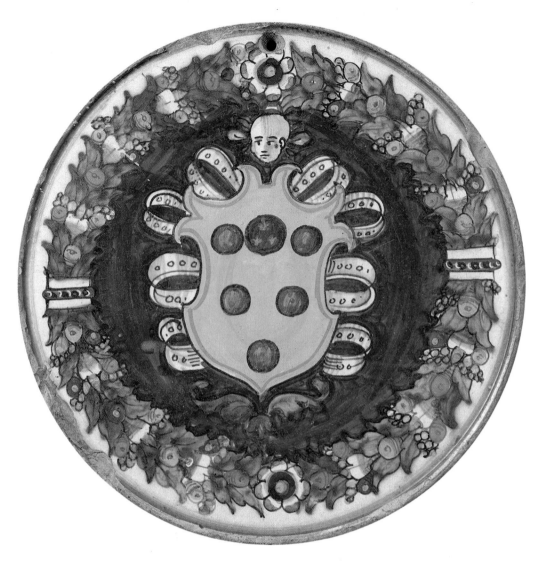

moral values of people living in community with each other. Both works also condemn privileged life at royal courts and in the higher realms of the Catholic Church, which they depict as being preoccupied with wealth, social status, and unnecessary displays of splendor.

The New Virtuous Citizen

In general, humanists argued that rulers should conduct affairs of state for the welfare of their subjects and believed that men and women could improve their own lot in life. Even Machiavelli, for example, believed that an unscrupulous and ruthless leader was more likely to be good at protecting his subjects than a weak king constrained by irrelevant moral considerations. Machiavelli's argument that society did not rely simply on one moral code governing rulers and subjects alike and that politics and power had their own morality marked a highly sophisticated view of the world.

Men and women, according to humanist thinking, should take an active part in the life of their communities. For the first time in many centuries, thinkers praised an active, balanced life in the world, as opposed to the contemplative life of a monk, who lived in isolation in a monastery. Monks in a sense turned their backs on the world, devoting their waking hours to the service of God. For humanists, citizens should take part in society, as they had in the days of ancient Greece and Rome.

For Machiavelli, too, the world was very different from that of the Christian monk. He ignored Christian virtues such as meekness, humility, and charity, substituting a more robust notion of practical virtue. The virtuous citizen was someone of ambition who wanted to get ahead in the world and was eager for the material blessings of life.

The virtuous citizen was also someone of valor, who placed a high value on duty to the state, loyalty, and patriotism. That notion of citizenship—of loyalty to the state rather than to the church—was still in its infancy. However, it was to grow in importance as Europe moved away from the concept of Christendom, which drew the whole continent together, toward its more modern form as a loose grouping of independent nation-states (*see 1:20*).

Social Structures

New Patterns of Life in Europe

Early modern Europe was characterized both by conflict between the continuation of traditional ways of life from the Middle Ages and the more or less gradual changes in society that heralded the coming of the modern age (*see 1:7*). Among the most disorienting changes were the rise of powerful monarchs and centralization of the state, rises in population, increased urbanization, rapid inflation, and the religious upheaval introduced by the emergence of Protestantism during the Reformation (*see 2:151*). Unrest spread throughout the continent as Europeans resisted change. Nobles revolted against the increasing authority of the king, the poor rebelled against the elites, and people fought relentless battles over religion.

This crown was made for the Austrian Habsburg emperor Rudolf II in 1602. Emerging monarchies often adopted elaborate ritual and luxurious regalia to enhance their royal status.

This Flemish painting from the 1580s shows a ball at the French court. Monarchs' courts increasingly attracted nobles who in feudal societies would have maintained their own local power bases.

The Nation-State

Among the most influential of the many changes was the gradual emergence of political entities that resembled modern nation-states instead of the feudal monarchies of the late Middle Ages. The feudal political system divided power between the king, nobles, and church leaders, called magnates. The king ruled only within a complex web of reciprocal feudal obligations. Although in theory his subjects owed him allegiance, the sovereign was not entitled to trespass on their rights and privileges. The apparatus and authority of the "state" therefore encompassed not only the monarch but also all the nobles, towns, provinces, and churches in the realm.

Centralized Monarchies

By 1560, France, Spain, and England had made great strides in unifying their territory, centralizing their administration, and magnifying royal power at the expense of the nobility. In the Holy Roman Empire, eastern Europe, and Italy, on the other hand, cities, nobles, and dukes retained power and autonomy, preventing the development of strong centralized states.

In 1589, the Italian political theorist Giovanni Botero published *On the Reason of State*. This influential work summed up the ethos of the centralized state. Botero argued that interests of state took priority over the medieval privileges of towns, nobles, church, or provinces. Monarchies should be governed only by their needs and goals and should be responsible to no one. The monarch was to be released from both secular and sacred restraints to rule through his council and offices of state. Although royal ministers could become powerful in their own right, their authority rested only on the king's. This relationship marked a change from the status of the monarch's traditional noble supporters, who possessed their own inherited authority.

Government and Religion

A major factor in the emergence of stronger monarchies was the religious change that came with the emergence of the Protestant confession to challenge the authority of the Roman Catholic Church. In France and Spain, monarchs aligned themselves with the established church and gathered support as defenders of the faith. In England,

on the other hand, the Tudor dynasty consolidated its hold on the throne by winning the loyalty of the Protestant nobility and middle classes against more conservative elements of society. Henry VII succeeded in identifying the monarchy with the national interest. His son, Henry VIII, established the Anglican Church, welding the dynasty more closely to Protestantism.

The Reformation had the opposite effect in the states of the Holy Roman Empire, or what is now Germany. Rather than help centralize authority, religious change tore the empire apart. Protestant lawyers, humanists, and political thinkers joined with local interests to revolt against the influence of the pope and ecclesiastical organizations. The upheaval also marked the end of the fading powers of the Holy Roman emperor, who proved unable to hold the country together. Local princes took control and strengthened their position and income by raising taxes on goods passing in to, out of, or through their territory. Germany was thus increasingly divided by customs and toll barriers.

Ideas of Social Discipline

The emergence of centralized monarchies required new thinking about social discipline, traditionally imposed at a local level by feudal lords or by peer pressure in a community. Monarchs depended on local administrators to carry out their will. In Spain, the Castilian crown appointed and paid a *corregidor* to oversee local affairs. To prevent these officials from identifying too closely with local interests, they could

Coats of arms, such as this French example from the sixteenth century, were essential symbols of rank in early modern society, which was obsessed by social status.

only spend five years in any one locality and could not serve in their home localities. At the end of the *corregidor*'s term, a judge visited the district to receive complaints and to prepare for the king's council a full report on the administration.

In England, the crown appointed justices of the peace to serve a similar function. Unlike the corregidors, however, they were not paid and served voluntarily—often they were wealthy landowners. Because they were volunteers, justices of the peace had more independence than the corregidors. When the interests of the crown conflicted with the justices' own class and local interests, the latter often prevailed.

Continuing Traditions

Medieval feudal ideas of government by consensual contracts did not die totally. In England and Holland, systems of parliamentary institutions developed despite monarchical opposition. In England, Parliament began to establish itself as the representative of the country's wishes. English kings realized that they could not raise high taxes without Parliament's consent, for example, although in many other respects, Parliament was firmly subordinate to the crown in the sixteenth century.

England also maintained what is called its common law, a countrywide system of justice that was based on tradition and precedent rather than laws decreed by king or Parliament. Henry VII found the common law useful in establishing monarchical authority and centralizing government. The survival of such traditional institutions in centralized states could work both ways, however. Opponents of the monarchy would come to see both the common law and Parliament as possessing independent authority that could be used to challenge royal power.

The Standing Armies

The emergence of monarchies brought the emergence of standing armies. Feudal magnates had hired temporary mercenary armies to wage private wars. In the sovereign state, waging war became a monopoly of the king. Some historians argue that the rise of the sovereign state is indivisible from the growth of royal armies. With a loyal army, the king could defeat unruly subjects and forcibly restore order.

The fifteenth- and sixteenth-century growth in trade and commerce and the establishment of efficient tax-collecting systems enabled European states to create large armies. Many monarchs poured more than half of their income into creating large forces to maintain their positions: five-sixths of the royal income in Spain was

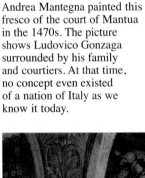

The Renaissance Italian artist Andrea Mantegna painted this fresco of the court of Mantua in the 1470s. The picture shows Ludovico Gonzaga surrounded by his family and courtiers. At that time, no concept even existed of a nation of Italy as we know it today.

spent on the army. Advances in technology and gunpowder made these armies more powerful—and more expensive to maintain—than any before.

Towns built elaborate fortifications to resist these modern armies. Fortifications were often built in star shapes to multiply the available angles of fire for defenders and make approach to the town difficult. To capture a town, an attacking army had to build trenches in order to bring its guns and cannons close to the walls. Attack and defense were both expensive and time-consuming, yet warfare remained almost constant throughout the early modern period.

The Merchant and Capitalism

Political and social changes in early modern Europe reflected profound shifts in economic life (*see 1:39*). The key figure in the changing economy was the merchant. In the late Middle Ages, the merchant had been a trader who traveled with his goods from place to place. Now, centralized states promised improved travel conditions, better routes, and greater security for goods. A form of marine insurance began, making shipping less risky. The merchant became a man in a shop, administering his suppliers and goods.

The merchant's pursuit of profit earned the disapproval of the traditional arbiters of social morality, the church and the aristocrats, for whom making money was ignoble. To be noble in the Middle Ages meant that one lived nobly and did not sully one's hand with work, even at the cost of falling into genteel poverty. Medieval theologians, meanwhile, decried the acquisition of wealth. The Catholic Church prohibited usury, or charging interest on loans.

Attitudes were beginning to change, however. In Italy, the humanists celebrated the positive qualities of wealth. Quoting classical authorities such as Aristotle's *Ethics* and *Politics*, they argued that wealth was a necessary attribute to the development of a moral and happy life. To make money through trade was fast becoming more respectable.

This sixteenth-century silver and wood model shows a merchant carrying his goods on his back. By the time this model was made, such a figure was already rather old-fashioned and rural. Urban merchants operated on a larger scale over longer distances and rarely hawked their goods.

Social Status

The development of wealth gradually undermined the feudal social structure. Strict attention to rank and status characterized social life in early modern Europe. A person's rank was evident in the style of clothing he or she wore or the crest displayed on his or her possessions, and in where he or she lived, went to school, marched in a procession, or sat in church. Europeans imagined that what was called a great chain of being stretched down from God to the lower forms of life, such as plants and minerals. Each thing had its carefully ordained place in the chain.

Society was similarly ordered, rising from the peasant to the highest noble to the king. Gentlemen, only a small fraction of the population, held an importance and influence out of all proportion to their numbers. They also possessed an immense proportion of their country's wealth and land, enabling them to become local officeholders and leading figures in their community.

The Nature of Nobility

The idea of a fixed social hierarchy was becoming increasingly difficult to maintain. There were new ideas about what constituted nobility, for example. Humanists argued that true nobility was found in personal virtue, exquisite manners, and nobility of spirit rather than in birth and inheritance. Most of the fifteenth-century humanists who advanced such ideas were Catholics living in traditional monarchies, but their arguments fit well with the moral values of the Protestant merchant class that had begun to dominate society in some European countries. For this class, the greatest sin was idleness and the greatest virtue thrift.

Many merchants, however, aspired to the status of the nobility. Thanks to the expansion of monarchical government, it became easier for men to enter high office by winning favor at court or by buying a position. Wealthy men bought offices and titles, invested in land, and married into impoverished noble families. Such social aspirations fed an interest in education. Under the influence of humanist thought, a gentleman was supposed to be well versed in all subjects. Across Europe, institutions of higher learning thrived as young men prepared for noble status.

The New Nobility

The emergence of a new nobility occurred in many places. English middle-class merchants made fortunes in the wool trade. They bought administrative offices for their sons, who bought up land and formed a new gentry. In France the pattern was similar. Middle-class merchants bought their sons offices in the royal administration. The son made his fortune in government, then bought land and a title. Even the family that ruled sixteenth-century Venice increasingly invested its wealth in land.

There were some countries in which the nobility remained more static, however. In

This French painting of 1590 shows a religious league on a procession through a town. Such religious processions were a regular feature of early modern life. Where a person marched in the procession depended on his or her social rank.

Spain and Poland, for example, well-established formal rules of lineage governed the makeup of the aristocracy and proscribed commercial activities. Newcomers to the nobility boosted the wealth of countries such as England and the Netherlands. The more restrictive nobilities, such as the Spanish *hidalgos*, although apparently more secure, became impoverished and, ultimately, redundant.

The Lower Classes

The opportunity to increase one's income and status remained limited, even where no formal rules restricted movement between social classes. The lower classes were often oppressed by heavy taxes as landowners sought to increase their own revenue to support noble lifestyles. Food prices were high, and the poor suffered disproportionately from famine and disease. Some escaped to the city, but many also endured dreadful poverty there. A lucky few became apprentices and earned a decent living as craftsmen. Others joined Europe's rapidly growing armies. Soldiers were frequently ill fed and ill paid, however, and armies were hotbeds of disease.

The Family

The fundamental economic division of society was the family. Husband and wife worked together as an economic unit to which their children also contributed labor. The family provided a metaphor for political and social order. Conventional thought held that the king was a father to his people and a father was king of his household. The ordering of the familial household reflected the ordering of village, county, and state. The father, like the king, was supposed to protect and govern his family in exchange for obedience and respect.

Women's Lives

Life was especially hard for working women, who worked at home or in the fields. They rarely left their village. A woman's mother or an older female of her household taught her the skills that would enable her to run a household capably when she married or entered domestic service. Peasant girls learned the care of chickens, milking, cooking, brewing, and other domestic chores at a young age. They also went out in the fields to plant, weed, and help bring in the harvest.

Painted around 1600 by a Flemish artist, this picture shows women spinning and weaving wool. The flourishing woolen industry in Flanders gave many employment opportunities to women, who were traditionally responsible for spinning.

In the city, a wife would often combine her domestic responsibilities with helping her husband in the shop that was customarily attached to their home. Men and women did not normally perform the same tasks. Women tended to be responsible for spinning, for example. Marriage was thus mutually advantageous for both partners, because each was trained and conditioned for different economic activities that complemented each other. Marriage brought such economic advantages that those widowed soon remarried. Life for single women was very uncertain. They either lived with family members or earned a livelihood from temporary labor.

Village Life
Three-fourths of Europe's population lived in small villages where local government depended on close cooperation of both the governed and the governors, as it had under the feudal system. Gradually, the economic boom of the sixteenth century began to loosen the tight structure and bonds of the traditional village. Richer peasants moved into the ranks of the middle class while urban merchants began to make inroads into the enclosed economic life of the village. In England and the Netherlands, for example, urban entrepreneurs organized the production of wool on a new scale in the putting-out system. Traditionally, villages that raised sheep had also woven their wool. Now, the urban merchants bought raw wool in sheep-rearing areas and sent it to other villages, those geared to weaving and producing cloth for sale.

Life in the City
Gradually, rural life became increasingly tied to urban life, especially as many country people began to migrate to the growing towns and cities. Many were driven out by poverty and attracted by the lure of growing rich. There was hardly a family that did not have some member struggling to make it in the big city.

Many local nobles also left the country for city life, relying on their estates only as a source of income. The city, especially the capital cities of newly centralized states, offered them social prestige, a better chance in the marriage market, and very frequently, the opportunity to secure a profitable government office. No longer were nobles content to draw their status from the antiquity of their titles or the extent of their holdings. They saw service to the throne, royal favor, and government office as their best sources of power and influence.

Nobles and the State
Power came at a price. The nobility gradually forfeited military and monetary independence in return for tax exemptions and

This 1609 painting shows an idealized view of life in a Dutch village beside a canal. Although most Europeans still lived in villages, the traditional social patterns that held communities together were beginning to break down.

This aerial photograph shows houses in a town square in Riga, in modern Latvia. The process of urbanization did not only affect western Europe. The stimulus of trade also led to the growth of sizable towns in eastern Europe, particularly in the Baltic states.

This early sixteenth-century book illustration from France shows shops lining the streets of the capital city, Paris. Capital cities emerged as particular focuses for population attracted by the wealth of monarchical courts.

aristocratic privileges. As the needs of the state grew more complex, however, it, in turn, needed nobles to run its bureaucracy. They alone possessed the education, experience, and status to run the state. Throughout most of early modern Europe, the nobles were the dominant social group.

By 1550, Europe's nobility was a group apart. Its members felt themselves superior and were so recognized by society. Across Europe, nobles commanded attention, obedience, and admiration; they were accorded special legal and economic privileges, very often accompanied by a title.

The Shape of the Village

The nobility distanced themselves from the villagers who had been in their personal care only a century earlier. Charity was seen as no longer a neighborly duty but the responsibility of the church or government. The church, too, was changing. Under the influence of the Reformation and Catholic reform, parish priests were becoming better educated. They were increasingly obliged to inculcate authentic doctrine in their parishioners, denouncing folk beliefs as superstitious or heretical.

As state administration expanded, villagers encountered a series of tax collectors, recruiting officers, and other officials. Villagers had a new importance as a supplier of manpower and as a tax base, besides being the producers of food and raw materials, such as wool. Villages were no longer isolated and self-sufficient. Everywhere they were being absorbed by the developing territorial states.

The Renaissance and the Arts

A Creative Flowering in Europe

The use of the word *Renaissance* is often disputed by historians who object to attaching names to periods in history long after the events took place. They point out that people living at the time often did not use such names and would probably not have understood them. They also argue that naming periods implies that history can be broken into clean, separate sections rather than being a continuum. Nevertheless, the word is still popularly applied to the flowering of artistic activity in the fifteenth and sixteenth centuries, particularly in Italy. *Renaissance* is a French form of the Italian word *rinascita*, which means "rebirth." The rebirth in question was that of western

Europe's classical heritage of writers, artists, and thinkers who lived in pre-Christian ancient Greece and Rome.

Living in a New Age
While historians may be right to emphasize that history is a continuous process rather than a series of separate ages, the Renaissance is a case where contemporaries would understand the meaning of the label. Some people living at the time did believe that they were entering a new age, breaking with the medieval past, and forging a link with classical times. Early in the fifteenth century, the German cleric Nicholas of Cusa (1401–1464) was already referring to

The dome of San Lorenzo Church rises above present-day Florence, in Italy. Designed in 1421 by the architect Filippo Brunelleschi (1377–1446), San Lorenzo was commissioned by the Medici family, the leading artistic patrons of contemporary Florence.

79

In this painting, the early Renaissance artist Masaccio shows Saints Peter and Paul. Drawing on techniques developed by relief sculptors, Masaccio not only portrayed biblical characters as individuals but used draped clothing, light and shadow, and perspective to give the human figure a solid rather than a flat form.

The Florentine Leon Battista Alberti (1404–1472) built the facade of the Church of Santa Maria Novella in his hometown. Alberti adopted the Roman triumphal arch for the main doorway.

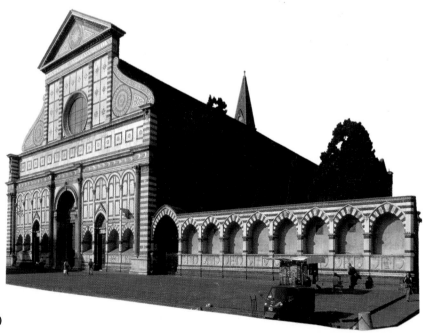

the centuries between the fall of the Roman Empire and his own time as the *media tempus*, or Middle Ages. The word *Renaissance* was used by men of arts and sciences to describe their own time.

Recent historians, however, are careful to point out that the concept of the Renaissance remains flawed. The period did not see a sudden transition from the "backward" Middle Ages to enlightened attitudes. The city-states that supported the great artists were also home to enduring superstition and intolerance. Punishment for wrongdoers was often harsh. Disease, unemployment, and poverty made the lives of most people miserable and short. Violence was endemic as states fought each other and nobles vied for power within states. In Rome, baronial supporters who inadvertently strayed into a part of city dominated by a different baron risked being attacked or murdered by rivals and their bodies thrown into the Tiber River. Privilege, factionalism, and cronyism dominated politics, religion, and everyday life.

The Influence of Florence

The Renaissance began in the fourteenth century in the Italian city-state of Florence, the first center of Renaissance humanism. For centuries, the Roman Catholic Church had taught people that the highest goal in life was to withdraw from material temptation in favor of contemplation of divine truths. The Florentine humanists put forward an alternative view (*see 1:62*). They did not believe that taking an active part in the world, having material ambitions, or amassing riches were wrong. The humanists emphasized education in the humanities, or human sciences, to prepare young men for an active life in the community.

Arts, Patrons, and Wealth

The humanist view of education reflected the thriving commercial life of the Italian city-states. The accumulation of wealth in Italy is one reason why artistic creativity began to blossom there. Italy's rich—princes, bankers, and merchants—were eager to advertise their wealth and status by becoming the patrons of artists and architects. They collected libraries, too, at a time when the earliest printed books were themselves luxury artifacts and vied to engage the services of the most renowned scholars.

Painting, sculpture, and architecture had a much wider popular appeal than scholarship. The wealthy families of Florence paid artists to decorate their private chapels. These private chapels were built in small alcoves off the side aisles of churches. They gave the wealthy a chance to demonstrate both their status and their piety in the value of the decorations and ornaments.

Artists painted frescoes either directly onto the plaster of the walls or onto can-

vases or panels to hang on the walls, especially above the altar. Many experts believe that the Renaissance in painting was heralded by frescoes painted in a family chapel in the church of Santa Maria del Carmine in Florence. The frescoes, painted by Tommaso di Masolino (1383–c. 1447) and Tommaso Masaccio (1401–1428), marked a change in religious art. Christian art of the Middle Ages, represented mainly in stained-glass windows or in illuminated manuscripts, was dedicated to the worship of God. It rarely depicted individual features in human figures, and the paintings were executed with no attempt to give a three-dimensional effect, so that they appeared flat. Masaccio, following the example of the Florentine artistic pioneer Giotto di Bondone (1266/1276–1337), set out to give a picture an impression of spatial depth into which objects appear to recede. Arranging a picture in this way is known as giving a painting perspective.

Perspective was carefully worked out by geometry, the study of shapes. The discovery of how to do this, attributed to the Florentine architect Filippo Brunelleschi (1377–1446), was one of the most powerful influences on art. Perspective remained central to all painting until it was abandoned, in the late nineteenth century, by Cézanne (*see 6:843*) and later by the abstract painters of the twentieth century.

Continuity of Subjects

The art of the Renaissance did not much change the Christian emphasis. Most paintings still told stories from the Bible. Such a representative artist of the time as Leonardo da Vinci (1452–1519) created *The Last Supper*, depicting Christ's last meal before his crucifixion. Another great Italian artist, Michelangelo (1475–1564), created a monumental sculpture of David, the slayer of Goliath and the king of Israel, and a series of three beautiful *Pietà*s showing the Virgin Mary with the crucified Christ.

Alongside the continuing Christian tradition, however, were themes taken from antiquity. The David statue itself reflects the style of classical Greek sculpture and reveals a detailed knowledge of anatomy.

Michelangelo completed this tomb for Pope Julius II in 1545. In their concern to leave lasting monuments, religious and secular leaders displayed a concern with the future, a characteristic of humanist and Renaissance thought that was relatively modern.

Sculptor Andrea del Verrochio created this equestrian statue of the Venetian general, Bartolomeo Colleoni. Such statues not only advertised the martial skills of their subjects. In their careful balancing of the statue's weight on only two or three legs, they also displayed the sculptor's technical ability.

Michelangelo introduced a variety of movements in his depictions of the human body. He was the first artist of modern Europe to reveal the body in a range of different poses. Raphael (1483–1520), one of the finest High Renaissance artists, painted a huge canvas in praise of Greek learning and culture, *The School of Athens*, in which philosophers, led by Plato and Aristotle, are set against majestic Greek architecture.

Another development of artistic subject matter came when powerful people began to have their portraits painted so that future generations should remember them. When people sponsored religious paintings, they often had themselves and even their prize possessions included. Carved tombs, too, were a popular form of commemoration. Leonardo made a statue of his Milanese patron, Duke Francesco Sforza (1401–1466), seated on his horse. Such equestrian statues became fashionable, because they showed princes in a flattering pose.

The Concept of the Artist

The concept of a famous artist whose name would be remembered was itself quite new. Before the Renaissance, artists were considered simply skilled craftspeople, rather like carpenters or bricklayers. Few people knew, or much cared, who had designed a particular stained-glass window or carved church pews or even who the architects of cathedrals were. It did not matter in the

Middle Ages who made art; what mattered was that it was made for the glory of God. Everyone in medieval society had the same purpose in life: to live according to divine will and thus to glorify God (*see 1:7*).

There was no place in the medieval scheme for an individual genius who gave free rein to inspiration. In the Renaissance, however, an interest in fame and celebrity was shared by artists and their patrons. This is the most modern aspect of the period. Patrons did not simply wish to display their wealth, although that was important. Above all, they wished to be remembered after their death. How better than to have their likenesses preserved for posterity?

From Public to Private Art

Art had in the past been essentially a public activity. Stained-glass windows and the biblical narratives painted on church walls were there for all to see. During the Renaissance, the cultivation of artistic taste became far more a private matter. The quantity of art objects to be found in the private homes of the rich was far greater in 1500 than it had been a century earlier.

The greatest patron of the early Renaissance was Cosimo de' Medici (1389–1464), head of the banking family that controlled Florence. Cosimo ruled the city in the mid–fifteenth century and helped make it a center of humanist learning and the arts. He built and restored convents and churches. Cosimo's example was followed by his grandson, Lorenzo de' Medici (1449–1492), called "the Magnificent," who became ruler of Florence in 1469. Lorenzo was a humanist poet and a collector of antique manuscripts and works of art. Artists who wished to learn from classical models depended upon such collectors, without whom they would not have had the chance to see examples of the ancient art they so much admired.

Papal Patronage

In Rome, the most important patrons of the arts were the popes. Early in the fourteenth century, the papacy had established a tradi-

God's hand meets Adam's in the moment of the creation of humankind in this detail from the ceiling of the Sistine Chapel. Painted by Michelangelo from 1508 to 1512, the ceiling frescoes are one of the great monuments of Western art.

tion of bringing learned humanists to the Vatican court. Rome itself was a decaying city until Martin V, pope from 1417 to 1431, began to rebuild it. The program was continued by his successors, most notably Julius II (1443–1513). In the first two decades of the sixteenth century, Julius commissioned the architect Donato Bramante (1444–1514) to redesign the basilica, or cathedral, of St. Peter's in Rome, which is now part of the Vatican.

Julius also collected ancient statues and artifacts that had been excavated in Rome, enlarging artists' store of sources from classical times. Julius, too, commissioned Michelangelo to make his tomb and to decorate the ceiling of the Vatican's Sistine Chapel, which remains one of the outstanding achievements of the Renaissance.

Vibrant Venice

The Renaissance did not come to every Italian city-state at the same time. Until the late fifteenth century, it had barely touched Venice. Then, however, the city blossomed into a center of the book trade. In the next century, Venice entered a golden age of painting: the city was graced by such outstanding artists as Titian (c. 1485–1576), Giorgione (1476/8–1510), Tintoretto (1518–1594), and Veronese (1528–1588).

Venice was also Italy's most important center for music. More than other city-states, Venice staged spectacular religious and secular festivals to mark the seasons of the year and the great events in the Chris-

tian calendar. Such celebrations usually included the performance of choral works in the Cathedral of San Marco. Venice was home to Claudio Monteverdi (1567–1643), often called the father of modern European music. In the early years of the seventeenth century, Monteverdi composed some of the first ever operas. Most of them have been lost, but two of the three that survive, *Orfeo* and *The Coronation of Poppea*, are landmarks in the history of European music.

The Renaissance Ideal

The greatest single figure of the Renaissance was probably Leonardo da Vinci, who is most famous for his haunting painting of the *Mona Lisa*, with her enigmatic smile. Leonardo was the greatest representative of the all-round person who was one of the ideals of the Renaissance.

Leonardo was born in Vinci, a small town near Florence, in 1452 and died at Cloux, near Amboise, France, in 1519; his life spans almost exactly what art historians call the High Renaissance, the period when artistic achievement was at its height. From the age of fourteen, Leonardo was apprenticed to an artist and goldsmith, and by the age of twenty, he was one of the leading painters in Florence.

He was much more than a painter, however. When, at the age of twenty-nine, he applied for employment to Lodovico Sforza in Milan, he listed the accomplishments he thought would appeal to a new ruler eager to establish himself in unstable times: the building of light, strong, fire-resistant bridges for the easy movement of troops; a method for removing water from military trenches; and the design of guns, mortars, and artillery-proof chariots.

Even an artist such as Leonardo carefully flattered Sforza's vanity: "In time of peace I believe I can give perfect satisfaction and to the equal of any other in architecture and the composition of buildings public and private... I can carry out sculpture in marble, bronze, or clay, and also I can do in painting whatever may be done, as well as any other, be he who he may. Again, the bronze horse may be taken in hand, which is to be the immortal glory and eternal honor of the prince your father of happy memory, and of the illustrious house of Sforza."

Leonardo was both an artist and a military engineer. He was a scientist who dissected birds and animals and noted the action of gravity, although he did not understand its cause. He anticipated the discovery that blood circulated in the body and envisioned machines that could fly.

The outstanding Venetian artist Titian illustrated the Greek myth of *Bacchus and Ariadne* in this painting from about 1522 or 1523. Like other Venetian painters, Titian was renowned for his vibrant use of color.

Authorized by the seal of Prince Cesare Borgia, this parchment document from about 1502 commissioned Leonardo da Vinci to design fortifications in the Romagna region of Italy. Leonardo sold his services to Italy's princes as a military engineer as much as he did as an artist.

Leonardo's *Mona Lisa,* from about 1503 or 1505, is one of the most famous paintings in the world thanks largely to the artist's remarkable portrayal of his subject's enigmatic smile.

The Renaissance in the North

In Leonardo, Italy produced the characteristic figure of the Renaissance in the visual arts. In music, however, Italy was rivaled, if not eclipsed, by Flanders, a part of modern Belgium that was part of the duchy of Burgundy and later of the Habsburg Empire. Singers trained in Flemish cathedrals and in those of northern France were sought after throughout Europe.

Like painters, musicians saw their status rise during the fifteenth century. Like painters, too, musicians depended on the patronage of the rich and powerful for advancement. The Flemish composer Orlando di Lasso (1532–1594) was born in Mons in Flanders. Thanks to his beautiful voice, the young man was taken into the service of the viceroy of Sicily, in southern Italy. He prospered after he gained favor with Duke Albrecht of Bavaria, in whose service he spent most of his adult life as a composer. He was ennobled and made a knight of the Golden Spur by the pope in 1574 for his contribution to church music.

Musical Instruments

The most common musical instruments from the early fourteenth century to the late sixteenth were lutes and viols. Both were stringed instruments; lutes were plucked like a guitar, and viols played with a bow like members of the violin family. The Renaissance fiddle was an early forerunner of the modern violin.

Keyboard music, meanwhile, was written chiefly for the organ and the harpsi-

This miniature book illustration, painted in Bavaria in the 1560s, shows the Flemish composer Orlando di Lasso and the choir of the Bavarian Hofkapelle.

polyphonic form, each voice follows its own melody while blending with the voices around it. Masters of the polyphonic style such as Lasso and Monteverdi wrote hundreds of madrigals.

Writing Music

The invention of the printing press that helped the spread of vernacular literature (*see 1:60*) was also of great benefit to musical composers. They could become famous in many countries because their compositions could be published for people to perform in distant places. Music printing also acted as a spur to the development and standardization of musical notation, the method of writing down what musical performers should play or sing. The modern form of notation, the one still in use today, was not, however, fully developed until after the Renaissance.

This *lira da braccio*, ornamented with a carved representation of a male face, was made in Verona in 1511. The lira, a bowed instrument, was a forerunner of the modern violin.

chord, although near the end of the period the clavichord made its appearance. The clavichord resembled the modern piano, in that its strings were sounded by being struck with hammers rather than plucked, as were the strings in a harpsichord.

Religious and Secular Music

Music had traditionally been written for the church, both for regular services and for special occasions. The outstanding Italian church composer was Palestrina (c. 1525–1594). In nearly a hundred masses for the church, Palestrina brought the medieval tradition of polyphonic church music to its height. *Polyphonic* means "many voices," and polyphonic music has a number of separate melodic lines that are played or sung at the same time to create a shifting, harmonious combination.

Music was also increasingly written for secular occasions such as ballets and other entertainments performed at princely courts. The most popular songs of the period, called madrigals, were written for a number of voices or parts. In a madrigal, a

Vasari and the Artists

One of the most influential developments in the changing status of the artist in the fifteenth and sixteenth centuries was the publication in 1550 of a work still commonly known as *The Lives of the Artists*. The book, a collection of biographies of painters, sculptors, and architects, was the work of a painter and architect called Giorgio Vasari (1511–1574). Vasari's work remains a storehouse of information about the personalities and methods of Renaissance artists. Its most profound influence, however, was its promotion and consolidation of the new Renaissance attitude toward creators. No longer would they be anonymous craftsmen on the same level as woodcarvers or stonemasons. From the time that Vasari published his work, the lives, thoughts, and personalities of creative artists have become accepted as an essential interest for any cultured person. Although Vasari's first edition of his work highlighted architects over sculptors, he altered the order for the second edition eighteen years later. In this, too, Vasari was influential in assigning painting the primacy in the visual arts that it still enjoys.

Vasari's work as probably the earliest of all art historians overshadows his own achievements as an artist and an architect. Born near Florence in Tuscany, Vasari enjoyed the patronage of the Medici family for much of his life. *The Lives of the Artists* was dedicated to Grand Duke Cosimo of Florence (1519–1574). For the Medici, Vasari also painted fresco cycles in the Palazzo Vecchio in Florence and designed the city's Uffizi Palace.

The Lives of the Artists both reflected the cultural environment in which Vasari lived and perpetuated it for the future. It reflected the common humanist view of the Middle Ages as a dark age in Europe that produced no cultural achievements of any worth. That attitude, too, colored those of successive generations of Europeans. Like his contemporaries, Vasari looked back to the classical antiquity of Greece and Rome for his artistic ideals.

Vasari's chief concern is to celebrate the revival of the classical arts in Tuscany. He dates the revival to the works of the artist and architect Giotto (1266/1276–1337). Giotto painted early cycles of frescoes, particularly in the Church of St. Francis in Assisi, and also designed the

famous bell tower and facade of the cathedral in Florence. Giotto's work, Vasari argues, launched an artistic progression that culminated in the works of Michelangelo, who was the only living artist mentioned in the first edition of *The Lives of the Artists*.

The enlarged second edition of the work contained numerous biographies of Vasari's contemporaries, as well as the author's own autobiography. These stories are some of historians' major sources of information about the Renaissance. Vasari writes in a readable, almost chatty style, not bothering to disguise his own prejudices and relating entertaining or scurrilous anecdotes about his subjects. Experts comparing Vasari's accounts to other contemporary records have concluded that he did not hesitate to make up facts where he needed to. Nevertheless, in terms of its influence, *The Lives of the Artists* remains one of the most important books about art ever written.

Portrait of a Young Man with a Medal was painted in about 1475 by the Florentine artist Sandro Botticelli (1445–1510). Vasari, whose work provides the only information about Botticelli's early life, praised the artist for the quality of "grace" in his paintings.

A crowning achievement of the northern Renaissance, *The Ambassadors* was painted by Hans Holbein the Younger in 1533. The portrait shows two French ambassadors at the English court, carefully displayed with a range of objects that reinforce their scholarly and cultural interests and achievements. In the foreground, Holbein has painted a distorted skull that only looks normal if it is viewed from one side, at an angle. The skull is not only a typical reminder from the period that the glories of life will all end in death. It is also a deliberate display by the artist of his formidable technical skill.

The Northern Renaissance

It was not just in music that northern Europe played its part in the Renaissance. Although the influence of the new styles in painting and architecture did not reach Germany, France, the Netherlands, and England until about a century after they had come to the fore in Italy, they had a profound influence when they did arrive.

One of the first northern artists to feel the influence of Italian culture was Albrecht Dürer of Nuremberg (1471–1528), who traveled to Italy a number of times. Talented in painting and engraving, Dürer produced old-fashioned religious woodcuts that allowed him to find the largest possible audience for his prints. Dürer also painted panels and made woodcuts of secular subjects in a more modern Renaissance manner. He was one of the earliest artists to portray himself in a series of self-portraits.

In the Netherlands the greatest example of the new painting was Hans Holbein the Younger (1497/8–1543). In the early sixteenth century, Holbein painted highly individual portraits of his patrons, notably King Henry VIII of England, for whom he worked for a number of years as an official court painter. Other Dutch and Flemish artists developed a tradition of painting religious or biblical scenes in a contemporary setting. They portrayed glimpses of daily life in the increasingly urban Low Countries in the background of their pictures. Later, such scenes moved to the foreground as a characteristic expression of urban pride in the Low Countries.

The French Renaissance

The most lasting French contribution to the Renaissance proved to be the luxurious châteaus, or palaces, built in the first half of the sixteenth century during the reign of Francis I (1494–1547), who attracted many Italian artists and musicians to his court. Italian and French architects and craftsmen combined to create the royal complex at Fontainebleau. Although they retain French hallmarks such as dormer windows and steep roofs, the buildings also reflect the classical forms of the Italian Renaissance. Thanks to printing, traveling artists, and the diffusion of culture by word of mouth, the style of the Renaissance had, in barely more than a century, become dominant virtually everywhere in western Europe.

The Margins of Europe

Poland and Russia

Sixteenth-century buildings line a square in the town of Telc, now in the Czech Republic. Although the towns of central Europe reflected the region's prosperity, such urban centers were rare in eastern Europe because of the power of the landed nobility there.

Central and eastern Europe marked the boundary between the Roman Catholic, Latin world of western Europe and the Orthodox Christian world of the Byzantine empire. By the Middle Ages, the region was occupied by a people known as the Slavs. The South Slavs included the Serbs, Croats, Bulgars, and others who settled in the Balkan Peninsula of southeast Europe. The other main groups were the West Slavs, who became known as the Poles and Czechs, and the East Slavs, who emerged as Russians and Ukrainians.

In the ninth century, the arrival of the Magyars—or Hungarians—who spoke an entirely different language, cut the South Slavs off from the other Slavs. As a result, their history developed differently from that of the East and West Slavs. From the fourteenth to the early twentieth century, their history was closely bound to that of the Ottoman Turks who conquered the Balkans in the fourteenth century (*see 1:100*). The East and West Slavs, meanwhile, and their Hungarian neighbors, had more in common.

East and West

In the ninth century, the East Slavs came under the rule of Viking adventurers from northern Europe known as Varangians. Their leader, Rurik, established his headquarters at Novgorod in the north, but his successor moved the capital to Kiev, farther south, on the Dnieper River. The Varangians called these newly conquered lands Rus, from which comes the name of their empire, Kiev Rus, as well as the name Russia itself.

In time, the Varangians adopted the language of their Slavic subjects; they also received Christianity from Byzantium,

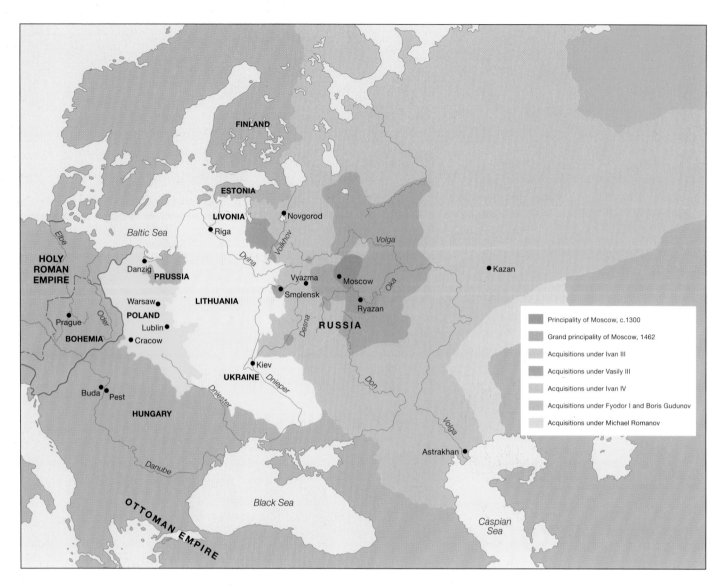

This map shows the major territorial divisions of eastern Europe and the expansion of Muscovy into Russia from about 1300 to about 1645.

together with Greek Byzantine culture, and a modified form of the Greek alphabet. In contrast, the West Slavs, who were not so close to Byzantium, received Christianity from Rome, as did the Hungarians. They also adopted the Latin alphabet and other aspects of Latin culture.

Latin and Byzantine Christianity began as different traditions within the same church, which was both Catholic—or "universal"—and Orthodox. However, after a dispute in 1054 between the pope and the Byzantine patriarch, the leader of the Orthodox tradition, the church split into two opposing factions, the western Roman Catholic Church and the eastern Orthodox Church, both claiming to represent true Christianity. As a result, the division between western Latin culture and eastern Byzantine culture, including that of Kiev Rus, grew deeper.

In the thirteenth century, Kiev Rus was overrun from the east by central Asians called the Mongols or Tatars. Much of southern Rus became part of the Mongol khanate of the Golden Horde; its princes

paid tribute to the Mongols. Rus was also invaded from the west by the neighboring Lithuanians, who helped reduce the region to a collection of weak duchies until the emergence of the grand duchy of Moscow in the late 1300s.

Lithuania and Poland

Toward the west, among those peoples who had absorbed Latin culture and the Catholic form of Christianity, the end of a long series of Crusades launched by Christendom against Islam in the Holy Land brought unexpected conflicts. In the early thirteenth century, a large group of Germanic warrior-monks known as the Teutonic Knights were invited by a Polish duke to help convert the pagan Prussians of northern Germany to the Christian faith. The fierce knights, veterans of the fighting in the Holy Land, easily conquered Prussia and turned it into a monastic, militaristic state. They then helped themselves to Polish territory on the shore of the Baltic Sea. In the fourteenth century, the Teutonic Knights turned their attentions to neighbor-

This nineteenth-century painting re-creates the 1410 Battle of Tannenberg between Poland-Lithuania and the Teutonic Knights. In the center of the picture rides the red-coated Vytautas, ruler of Lithuania.

ing Lithuania. Faced with the common threat to their territory, Poland and Lithuania decided to unite.

A Joint Monarchy

Poland badly needed a strong ruler. In 1385 its monarch was a girl of eleven, Jadwiga, or Hedvig. In order to unite the two countries, the Polish lords persuaded her to marry Wladyslaw Jagiello (1351–1434), grand duke of Lithuania, who was still a pagan. He, in turn, agreed to be baptized into the Christian church in order to become king of Poland, which he ruled as Wladyslaw II from 1386 to 1434. This was the beginning of the influential Jagiello dynasty, which would rule Poland-Lithuania, Hungary, and Bohemia until the sixteenth century.

In 1401, Wladyslaw decided to allow his cousin, Vytautas (1350–1430), to rule as grand duke in Lithuania. As a result, over the next century, the king of Poland was often a different member of the same family as the grand duke of Lithuania. Thus, in this situation, the Jagiello dynasty ruled in Lithuania as hereditary grand dukes but in Poland as elected kings.

In the short term, the merger of the two countries had its desired effect. The com-

bined armies of Poland and Lithuania defeated the Teutonic Knights at the Battle of Tannenberg, also called the Battle of Grünwald, in 1410. Later, in the Thirteen Years' War (1454–1466), Poland recovered its lands on the Baltic coast from the Teutonic Knights. The war was fought by Casimir IV, the second of Wladyslaw's sons to follow him onto the Polish throne.

Casimir had been grand duke of Lithuania before he became king of Poland. He

The restored fifteenth-century castle of Trakai looks out over Lake Galve. In the fifteenth and sixteenth centuries, Trakai was the capital of Lithuania.

The Legacy of Byzantium

In 1453, Constantinople, capital of the Greek Byzantine empire and headquarters of the eastern, Orthodox branch of Christianity, fell to the Muslim Ottoman Turks. The repercussions were profound. Western thought was enriched by the arrival of scholars familiar with Greek and Arabic traditions. The Orthodox faith, meanwhile, found a new capital in Moscow, the "third Rome."

Christianity had arrived in Russia in the tenth century. Its pagan ruler, Vladimir, sent representatives to investigate various religions. They rejected Islam—supposedly because it forbade alcohol—and Roman Catholicism. From Constantinople, however, they reported: "We knew not whether we were in heaven or earth, for on earth there is no such vision nor beauty, and we do not know how to describe it; we know only that there God dwells among men." Vladimir adopted the Orthodox religion in Kiev Rus, marrying a Byzantine princess and forcing his subjects to convert to Christianity.

Kiev flourished as a Christian capital. It was particularly distinguished by beautiful churches built in Greek traditions. Most of these churches were wood, however, and they do not survive. After the centuries during which Kiev fell to Mongol rule, the rise of Muscovy saw Moscow inherit the same tradition of church building. The characteristic onion-shaped domes of the Greek church are still a familiar sight in Moscow.

The end of the fifteenth century saw Ivan III create a splendid capital to rival Rome and Constantinople. He redesigned the Moscow Kremlin, the fortified city that was the center of government. At its heart, a large square was home to four more or less brand new cathedrals. Ivan replaced his traditional wooden palace with the Palace of the Facets, named for the diamond-cut stones of its facade.

Calculations by Orthodox theologians had predicted that the end of the world would come in 1492, which they believed was the end of the seventh millennium of creation. No one even bothered to calculate the church calendar for that year. For the metropolitan, or archbishop, of Moscow, these calculations became a pressing priority. When the metropolitan published the new calendar in 1492, he first identified Moscow as the new Constantinople—and Ivan III as the new emperor Constantine.

The Byzantine tradition held that church and state were indivisible. There could be no emperor without the faith and no true faith without an emperor. For forty years, however, there had been no emperor. Some people believed that Russia should look to Constantinople or even to the western Holy Roman Empire for an emperor. Others believed that Moscow must find its own emperor: Ivan III.

Although Russian tradition claims that Moscow simply inherited the Orthodox faith, the religion actually changed significantly. Byzantine traditions of architecture, art, and ritual were retained, but Russian Orthodoxy was far narrower than the universal Christianity of Byzantium. It linked the church to Russian nationalism and, via the activities of various monastic orders who grew rich through property, to land ownership. Orthodox theologians who claimed to protect the new faith helped begin a recurrent theme in Russian history: that evil came from the West.

This seventeenth-century church fresco from Russia shows Michael Romanov, founder of the Romanov dynasty, with his son Alexei, supporting an image of Christ. Such religious paintings, called icons, were inherited from Byzantium. The Orthodox Church saw religious icons as holy objects, worthy of reverence.

was therefore able to unite the countries more closely than before. He also formed the first Polish parliament, called the *sejm*, and laid the groundwork for Poland's development in the sixteenth century.

The Jagiello Dynasty

When Casimir IV died in 1492, he had added considerably to the strength of his family not just in Poland and Lithuania but throughout the region. After his death, three of his sons reigned over a third of Europe. The eldest, Ulászló II, was king of Bohemia and Hungary; John I Albert was king of Poland; and Alexander was grand duke of Lithuania.

Challenge from the Habsburgs

The power of the Jagiello rulers was challenged by another mighty family, the Habsburgs. The Austrian Habsburgs had amassed their own empire and were also regularly elected Holy Roman emperors, or rulers of the German empire. The two dynasties agreed that the Habsburgs would inherit Bohemia and Hungary if the Jagiello line there died out, as it soon did: Louis II, king of Hungary and Bohemia, was killed by the Ottoman Turks at the Battle of Mohács in 1526. The crowns were inherited by Ferdinand of Habsburg (1503–1564)—later the Holy Roman emperor Ferdinand I—though not without problems. The Turks occupied much of Hungary, and in 1529, they laid siege to the Austrian capital, Vienna, itself.

Although eventually driven back from Vienna, the Turks held on to eastern and central Hungary. In the eastern province of Transylvania, they allowed local Hungarian princes to rule under their authority, but in the country's heartland, the Turks ruled directly. Turkish rule was a disaster for Hungary, culturally and economically. For the Habsburgs, the death of Louis may have given them the rich kingdom of Bohemia but it also brought the burden of defending Europe from the Turks.

Prosperity in Central Europe

The wars in central Europe did not prevent a steady growth in the region's population, the amount of land farmed, and the number and size of towns. Nor was this growth interrupted by the Black Death, the plague that devastated western Europe at the time. Indeed, growth seemed to accelerate in the mid–fourteenth century.

Poland also benefited from its recovery from the Teutonic Knights of the city of Danzig—now called Gdansk—on the Baltic sea in 1467. Grain, timber, furs, and

other commodities were shipped in vast quantities from Danzig to the ports of northwest Europe. Danzig became the largest city in the region. The early sixteenth century also witnessed a stimulus to trade with the immigration of many Jews who were fleeing from persecution farther west, particularly in Spain. Protected by local rulers and noblemen, the Jews settled in towns and engaged in trade.

By the later sixteenth century, however, the economy of central Europe was becoming unbalanced. The area mainly exported raw materials and imported finished goods, many of them luxuries, which meant that local trades and industries did not grow. Most trade was in the hands of foreign merchants. Although towns continued to grow, therefore, most did not grow as fast as those in western Europe.

Another problem for economic development was that the nobility, especially in Poland, was trying to increase its political and economic importance. Noble families secured trade privileges that gave them an

This painting from 1515 shows the young king Louis II of Hungary. Louis died a decade later, fleeing the Ottoman defeat at the Battle of Mohács in 1526, the battle that marked the end of Europe's feudal armies of knights in armor.

A baked-goods merchant sells her wares in a fifteenth-century market in Bohemia in this contemporary drawing. Giant pretzels hang on the stand in the background.

peasants already owed their lords. This repression of the peasants is called "the second serfdom," because it occurred much later than the same process in western Europe, where by this time the feudal system was collapsing. In practice, the restrictions in eastern Europe were poorly enforced. Most peasants still had enough land to grow food to feed their families.

Religious and Cultural Developments

Prosperity brought an intellectual flowering, particularly after the foundation of the universities of Prague and Cracow in 1348 and 1364, respectively. The late fifteenth century saw the arrival of the Renaissance, as humanist scholars traveled to the region from Italy and Poles and Hungarians journeyed to Italy. The first printing presses appeared between the 1450s and 1470s, at the same time as in western Europe. Printing enabled people to read the Bible in their own languages, in turn helping Czech and Polish to emerge as respectable literary languages in their own right.

Just as central Europe escaped the Black Death, so it also escaped the pessimism that hung over the Catholic Church. The Christian thinkers of central Europe emphasized the importance of individual morality and questioned the pope's spiritual authority. In Bohemia, Jan Hus (c. 1372–1415), the rector of Prague University, asserted that the Bible had greater authority than the pope; he also denounced the corruption of the Roman Catholic Church and demanded services and Bibles in the Czech language.

Hus's views were outlawed by the Catholic Church, which burned him as a heretic at the Council of Constance in 1415. Hus's followers, called Hussites, rose in revolt against the Holy Roman emperor, Sigismund of Luxembourg, in 1419. The Hussites established their own national church, which was still in existence when the Protestant Reformation began in the early sixteenth century. Early Protestant reformers claimed Hus as a martyr for their own cause (*see 2:152*).

The Reformation in Central Europe

At first, the Protestant Reformation was successful in many Habsburg lands. The Habsburg family itself remained Catholic but tolerated Protestant worship in its territories, though some members of the family

advantage over merchants and towns-people. They restricted the movement of peasants, tying them to particular pieces of land and forcing them to work their lord's land several days a week beyond what the

This statue on the grounds of the royal palace in Budapest, Hungary, commemorates King Matthias Corvinus. In the fifteenth century, Corvinus built up the greatest kingdom of central Europe.

Žatec Sein offene gewappnete

This contemporary drawing, which has been torn at the bottom some time in its 500-year history, shows Jan Hus, in black, on his way to his execution in 1415. Hus's followers, the Hussites, formed the dominant religious group in Bohemia, which is now divided between the Czech Republic and Slovakia.

accepted the new faith more easily than others. One of the tolerant Habsburgs was Rudolf II, Holy Roman emperor from 1576 to 1612, who was interested in many things, including different religious opinions. His court in Prague was one of the intellectual centers of Europe. In contrast, Ferdinand II, emperor from 1617 to 1637, was determined to win his lands back for Catholicism. In 1618, he provoked the Protestant nobles of Bohemia into revolt, thereby starting the disastrous Thirty Years' War (1618–1648) (*see 2:225*).

The Hussites made few converts in Poland, which remained strongly Catholic but was also tolerant of other religions. Such tolerance was necessary in a country with a large Jewish population and with

eastern lands that were inhabited mainly by Christians of the Orthodox Church. In Poland-Lithuania generally, the Reformation won over most German-speaking townspeople to Lutheranism and about a fifth of the nobility to a more radical form of Protestantism called Calvinism. This proportion was even higher among the richer nobility.

The demands of the Reformation for religious freedom encouraged nobles to claim more rights from both the church and the king. These were granted with very little struggle, and many of the next generation of nobility lost interest and returned to Catholicism. Another factor may have been the link between Protestantism and the Renaissance. For some people, Protestantism appealed to the mind more than the heart. When the Renaissance gave way to the less intellectual baroque culture of the seventeenth century, according to this interpretation, Protestantism also declined.

The Rise of Moscow

Religious and cultural developments in the rest of Europe often bypassed the duchy of Moscow, known in the West as Muscovy. Despite its trade with northwestern Europe, the duchy remained in cultural isolation. During the fourteenth century, Moscow was simply one of many duchies of Rus paying tribute to the Tatars. The nearby city-state of Novgorod was much richer.

The dukes of Moscow expanded their lands and their influence cautiously. They exploited quarrels among their neighbors, made marriage alliances, bought new territory, and acted as tribute collectors for the Tatars. They prevented the subdivision of

The Cathedral of the Assumption, in the Kremlin in Moscow, was built by Ivan III in 1492 as part of his program to glorify the seat of Muscovite royal power.

the duchy by leaving nearly all of their lands to their eldest sons. From the Tatars, they adopted the custom of expecting unconditional obedience from their people and dealing severely with any signs of treachery or disobedience. In time, the duchy rose to be the most important in Rus, eventually becoming a grand duchy.

Ivan III (1440–1505), also called Ivan the Great, who ruled from 1462 to 1505, used the tactics of his predecessors, as did his son Vasily III (1479–1533), who ruled from 1505 to 1533. Both these men were more ambitious than previous grand dukes. Ivan married the niece of the last Byzantine emperor and adopted the title of czar, meaning "caesar." Under his influence, Muscovite writers began referring to Moscow as "the third Rome," placing the duchy in a direct line from Rome and Byzantium as the center of the church.

The Power of the Czar

In Byzantine tradition, the emperor was also the head of the church, responsible only to God. Ivan and Basil asserted their authority over the Orthodox Church in Moscow and gave the office of czar a sacred, priestly quality. They also claimed to be the heirs of the old state of Kiev Rus and so challenged Lithuania for most of its territory. These imperial and religious claims gave the czars a powerful sense of mission. They threw off Tatar overlordship, absorbed Novgorod, and seized a third of Lithuania. The grand duchy of Moscow soon became the state of Russia.

Ivan III and Basil III introduced new methods of government to manage their growing territories. Instead of using the old noble families, or boyars, they preferred to govern through offices, or chanceries, staffed by secretaries. They also gave out some of the lands they conquered to people who promised to supply soldiers in time of war. Inevitably, these policies were unpopular with the boyars. When Basil III died, leaving his three-year old son, Ivan, to succeed him, the boyars ran amok.

Ivan the Terrible

The feuds of the boyars made a deeply unfavorable impression on the young czar, Ivan IV (1530–1584). When he took power in 1547, Ivan ignored the boyars' advice and challenged their power. He took provincial government out of their hands, confiscated some of their lands, and created more chanceries.

Around 1560, Ivan IV probably became mentally unbalanced. He remained deeply religious, but his behavior became wildly

Dmitry, was eventually crowned czar after Boris's death in 1605. Dmitry, who is now also called False Dmitry, was backed by the Polish nobles and had a Polish wife, a fact that made him unpopular in Moscow. He was overthrown in 1606 by Basil Shuisky. Shuisky was challenged by a second false Dmitry, supported by the Poles and an army of rebellious peasants. In 1610, a Polish army occupied Moscow, where a group of boyars chose as their new czar Wladyslaw IV Vasa, son of the Polish king, Sigismund III.

The election caused immediate problems. Sigismund wanted the Russian throne for himself, but he refused to convert from the Catholic to the Orthodox faith, making him an unacceptable ruler for

The young Ivan IV sits surrounded by Russian boyars, or nobles, in this drawing from the sixteenth century. Ivan's experience of the nobles led him to suppress them harshly as an older ruler.

unpredictable. Faced with an uprising in Novgorod in 1570, he destroyed the city and had its citizens boiled in tar and then drowned in the river. He repeatedly purged the boyars, mutilating and executing those whom he accused of disloyalty. He let loose a group of licensed thugs called "children of darkness," who murdered boyars and confiscated their lands for Ivan's benefit. Such actions are one of the reasons that Ivan is known as "the Terrible."

In other respects, Ivan was an intelligent and learned man. Printing came to Moscow during his rule. In foreign affairs, Ivan extended Russian rule south to the Caspian Sea and east into Siberia. On a less successful note, he tried to capture Livonia on the Baltic Sea but failed after twenty years of war that cost the Russians dearly.

Russia's Time of Troubles

In 1584, Ivan was succeeded by his son, Theodore, a religious but weak leader. Theodore left much of the responsibility of government to his brother-in-law, Boris Godunov (c. 1551–1605). So, when Theodore died without an heir in 1598, Boris was elected czar by the assembly of the land, which was made up of clergymen, boyars, and representatives of towns.

Because Boris had no hereditary right to the throne, various pretenders started appearing, claiming to be members of the royal family. One pretender, who claimed to be Theodore's dead younger brother

This detail of a contemporary woodcut shows Ivan IV, known as Ivan the Terrible, as czar of Russia. In 1581, Ivan strangled his own son, another Ivan, in a fit of anger.

the Russian boyars. As negotiations dragged on, a resistance movement grew in the Russian countryside against the Poles and their boyar allies. The resistance movement recaptured Moscow in 1612. The following year, the assembly elected Michael Romanov (1596–1645) to be czar. He began the Romanov dynasty that would rule over Russia until the Bolshevik revolution of February 1917 (*see 7:909*).

Russian Expansion

Russia's political crisis coincided with social tension whose origins lay in reforms begun by Ivan III. In response to the czar's requirements to supply and equip soldiers, landowners demanded more work from their peasants; Ivan's wars also coincided with a series of bad harvests and plagues. Many peasants fled to outlying, sparsely inhabited regions, despite laws forbidding them to do so. The disorder of the 1600s led the peasants into a massive revolt.

The chaos had one positive outcome for Russia. It drove explorers and trappers eastward through the forests and inhospitable tundra of Siberia to reach the Pacific Ocean in 1637. Russia was now the largest empire in the world but not the strongest. In eastern Europe, that position was held by Poland-Lithuania.

The Polish-Lithuanian Commonwealth

In 1569, Poland and Lithuania united more permanently to form the Commonwealth of the Two Nations. During the 1560s, it had become clear that the last Jagiello king of Poland, Sigismund II Augustus (1520–1572), would not leave an heir and that the Polish-Lithuanian link might be broken. The most powerful Lithuanian lords did not want Lithuania to become part of Poland, although they needed Polish help to resist Russian ambitions. Many Polish nobles wanted to unite Lithuania to Poland more firmly in order to secure their freedoms, while Lithuanian boyars wanted to enjoy the same rights as Polish nobles. Sigismund Augustus overcame Lithuanian resistance to union at a joint Polish and Lithuanian parliament, held at Lublin in 1569. Poland and Lithuania were to share a common parliament and a common king and grand duke, elected by the nobility. Both countries would keep their separate laws, offices, treasuries, and armies.

The commonwealth was unique in Europe. It was a large state where supreme power was in the hands of a relatively large number of citizens: the nobility, who made up about 6 percent of the population. The nobles enjoyed many political, personal, and religious freedoms. Although they often quarreled with their elected kings, their leaders were on the whole public spirited, inspired as they were by the example of the ancient Roman Republic.

Toward the Future

By the early seventeenth century, central and eastern Europe was again menaced by the Ottoman Turks. The nobility everywhere was consolidating its power over the peasants and pushing the towns to the margins of political life. Tension between Protestants and Catholics was rising. It would explode in the Thirty Years' War, which would drive a further wedge between central and western Europe. In the east, meanwhile, Romanov Russia was poised to become the region's greatest power (*see 5:687*).

The Ottoman Turks

A Great Empire Emerges from Asia Minor

In 1453, Christian Europe suffered a calamitous blow in its southeastern corner. Constantinople, for ten centuries the greatest Christian city, the capital of the Greek Byzantine Empire, and headquarters of the Eastern Orthodox branch of Christianity, fell into Muslim hands. The city's conquerors were the Ottoman Turks, descendants of nomadic tribes of central Asia.

The Rise of the Turks

The rise of the Ottomans began in the late thirteenth century in Bithynia in northwestern Anatolia, in Turkey. At the time, the region's dominant power was another Turkish dynasty, the Seljuks, who in the eleventh century had invaded the Holy Land and captured Jerusalem, the holiest city in the world to Jews and Christians and home of a sacred Muslim shrine. For two

centuries, the Seljuks and their allies defended their acquisitions against Christian crusaders.

In the east, meanwhile, the Seljuks faced another threat. Mongol invaders' westward campaigns drove discontented refugees into the Seljuk state, which was already weakened by the presence of largely independent Turkoman peoples in its frontier districts. In 1243, a Mongol victory at Köse Dagh reduced the Seljuks to a vassal state. As Seljuk administration broke down, Turkoman amirs, or princes, established small principalities beyond Mongol control.

Early Ottoman Footholds

Among the amirs establishing realms was Osman (1258–c. 1326), founder of the Ottoman dynasty. Osman commanded a group of Turkish *gazi*s, fighters for Islam

An Ottoman sultan presented this lavish copy of the Koran to the city of Jerusalem in the mid–sixteenth century. The Koran is the foundation of the Islamic faith.

99

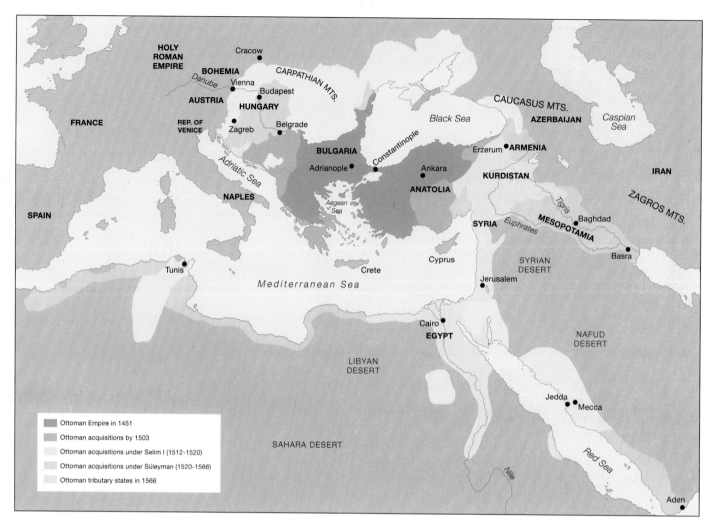

This map shows the emergence of the Ottoman Empire in the fifteenth and sixteenth centuries.

against the Byzantine Christians. In 1290, Osman proclaimed independence, offering land and plunder to mercenaries and refugees from the Mongols who would support him. By 1300, Osman had absorbed the small Christian territories around his kingdom, despite Byzantine attempts to reclaim them with mercenary troops.

Osman's successor, Orhan, consolidated Ottoman power by developing the apparatus of state government. He reduced his dependence on nomadic *gazi* fighters by hiring Christian mercenaries and moved to annex Turkoman territories to the south.

The Byzantine Empire

The rise of the Ottomans coincided with the decay of another great power, the Byzantine Empire. From its capital in Constantinople, now called Istanbul, the empire had once covered Greece, the Balkans, Asia Minor, and the Holy Land. Now it was reduced to little more than a city-state, however, weakened by the very crusading armies the emperor had summoned from western Europe to defend it from its Islamic neighbors.

Centuries of warfare had undermined the stability of imperial rule to the stage where

the Byzantines invited Ottoman interference in the empire. Orhan helped John VI Cantacuzenus win the Byzantine throne. In return, he married the emperor's daughter, beginning a tradition of contact between the Ottoman and Christian worlds. Orhan also won the right to plunder the wealthy province of Thrace, now part of Greece.

Destroying Byzantium

The raids into Thrace showed that the declining Byzantine Empire was ripe for plucking. In 1354, ignoring Byzantine protests, the Turks established a military base at Gallipoli on the narrow strait between the Mediterranean and the Black Sea. Bypassing the fortified capital of Constantinople, the Ottomans raided north into Thrace and the Balkan Peninsula. In 1361, they captured Adrianople, Byzantium's second city, which they renamed Edirne and made their capital. The city controlled the road north into the Balkans and thus Constantinople's main sources of grain and tax revenue. The Ottomans forced the Byzantine emperor to accept their suzerainty, or formal overlordship.

Despite European attempts to raise a crusade against the Ottomans, the Turks rap-

idly seized Macedonia, central Bulgaria, and Serbia in a campaign that ended with the Battle of Kosovo in 1389. The Ottomans established a pattern for their empire by creating a series of vassal states. Native rulers remained in place if they accepted Ottoman rule and paid annual tributes. Later, the Ottomans increasingly replaced vassal states with direct rule.

Bayezid I

The Battle of Kosovo marked a temporary limit of Ottoman expansion into Europe. When Bayezid I (c. 1360–1403) came to the throne in 1389, he turned to Anatolia, where the Ottomans had expanded their rule by means of dynastic marriages and by purchasing territory, to seize territory from his Turkoman neighbors. At the same time, he defeated Hungarian-led attempts to recapture the Balkans. Ottoman prestige had risen so high in the Islamic world that the caliph in Cairo—the spiritual leader of Islam—awarded Bayezid the title sultan, which had previously been reserved for the rulers of the Eygptian Mamluk dynasty.

Bayezid's success drew the attention of the Turkic leader Timur (1336–1405), who is also known as Tamerlane. Timur had established an empire that covered central Asia, Iran, Afghanistan, and modern Iraq. He was about to invade India, too, when he was distracted by growing Ottoman power. Urged on by Turkoman warlords defeated by the Ottomans, Timur invaded Anatolia. Bayezid's Muslim followers, meanwhile, had deserted him because he had abandoned the *gazi* tradition of holy war. Left only with an army of Christian vassals from the Balkans, Bayezid was defeated at Ankara in 1402. Taken captive, the sultan died a year later.

Restoring the Empire

Timur soon left Anatolia. He returned power to the Turkoman warlords, including Bayezid's sons, who began restoring Ottoman control. The process was completed by Murad II (1404–1451) and Mehmed II (1432–1482), who between them ruled the empire from 1421 to 1481.

Murad II restored Ottoman rule in Anatolia and the Balkans and fought the Ottoman's traditional ally, Venice, for control of the Adriatic Sea, the base of Venice's maritime trading empire. With the Venetians occupied by warring with their neighbors in Italy, the Ottomans built a

This fourteenth-century Byzantine manuscript illustration shows Arab troops attacking Messina, on the Italian island of Sicily. Arabs controlled the city from the ninth to the eleventh centuries.

The castle of Krak des Chevaliers looks out over a valley in Syria. The castle was built by European crusaders to protect the territory they had won from Muslim control.

fleet that enabled them to raid Venetian ports in the 1430s. This navy forced the Italian republic to accept an Ottoman presence in the Adriatic. In return, the sultan allowed the Venetians to become the leading commercial power in the empire.

Controlling the Notables
With the empire externally secure, Murad strengthened the Ottoman throne. The main threat to his power came from the notables, Turkish aristocrats whose support for the dynasty had won them land and power in Anatolia and the Balkans. To balance their influence, Murad built up the power of non-Turkish groups in his empire.

The bulk of these non-Turks were Christians from southeastern Europe who had been pressed into service. From them, Murad established an elite military corps called the Janissaries, who would exercise a profound influence on Ottoman society. Murad also instituted a system called *devshirme*, which recruited young Christians from the empire to convert to Islam and devote their lives to the sultan's service. Fearing the erosion of their power, the notables forced Murad to cease the campaigns into central Europe, which would increase the number of *devshirme*.

Mehmed II and Constantinople
In 1444, Murad retired to follow a religious life, passing the throne to his son, Mehmed II. The young king at once proved himself an able leader. His victory at Varna in 1444 against an alliance of Greeks, Hungarians, and Venetians ended the long sequence of European crusades against Islam.

At the urging of the *devshirme*, Mehmed attacked Constantinople in 1453. Using giant siege artillery designed by a Hungarian armorer (*see 1:26*), Mehmed overcame the city's once-impregnable defenses in only fifty-four days. The last Byzantine emperor, Constantine, died defending the city walls.

The capture of Constantinople brought the empire a suitably grand cultural and administrative capital, reflected in the opulent court of the Ottoman sultans. In 1453, the population numbered only some 100,000. Mehmed used tax concessions to draw talented people from all over the empire to repopulate the city. He allowed the newcomers to form their own self-governing communities, or *millets*, rather than force them to adopt Ottoman customs and Islamic beliefs. By 1600, the city had between 700,000 and 800,000 inhabitants, more than any European city of the time.

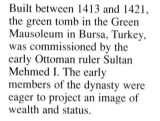

Built between 1413 and 1421, the green tomb in the Green Mausoleum in Bursa, Turkey, was commissioned by the early Ottoman ruler Sultan Mehmed I. The early members of the dynasty were eager to project an image of wealth and status.

This manuscript illumination, painted in France in 1455, shows the Ottoman forces at the fall of Constantinople two years earlier. The event sent a shock wave through Christendom.

Traditions of Government

Along with the new capital came a consolidation of imperial institutions. The Ottomans had long outgrown the traditions of government they inherited from their nomadic ancestors, though they still based their military organization on Turkic models. The Ottomans also drew on the models of their predecessors. From the Seljuks, they inherited a tradition of placing Islam at the heart of the state. From the Byzantine Empire, meanwhile, they developed a concept of the ruler as exalted and isolated, reflected in the adoption of elaborate hierarchies and court ceremonials.

In the Islamic world, spiritual power was meant to lie with the caliph and worldly power with the sultan, in the same way

This portrait of the Ottoman sultan Mehmed II is attributed to the Venetian artist Gentile Bellini. The Italian republic lent the painter to the sultan around 1479 in a gesture aimed at confirming the trading relations between Venice and the empire.

power was divided between the pope and the Holy Roman emperor in the Christian world. Under the Ottomans, however, the sultan came to combine both kinds of power as the religious and the political head of the empire.

A Meritocracy of Slaves

The Ottomans evolved an elaborate central administration divided into departments, each of which was directed by a vizier, or minister. The viziers gained great personal power as the sultans largely withdrew from the daily affairs of government.

Meanwhile, Mehmed stabilized the continuing struggle between the Turkish notables and the *devshirme*. He decreed that only people who accepted the status of slaves of the sultan could hold government or military positions. This bound all members of the ruling class, Turkish or otherwise, to the sultan's will. The Ottoman government would be an indivisible whole.

The sultan's servants could be Muslims or non-Muslims, so long as they agreed to devote their lives, possessions, and families to the sultan. Mehmed's system made the Ottoman administration a meritocracy in which talent alone could advance a career. In European countries political power lay with traditional noble elites, but the Ottoman system was open to anyone willing to accept its conditions.

In order to protect the sultan's personal power and guarantee the line of succession, Mehmed began a practice that became an Ottoman tradition. He executed all his brothers so that the succession would be limited to one of his sons. Future sultans went further, also executing all but the most able of their own sons.

Ottoman Power Grows

Even before Mehmed's decree, the empire had depended on slavery. The capture of Constantinople brought access to a vast new reservoir of slaves and food in the west. The Tatars of neighboring Crimea made extensive forays into Poland and Lithuania, rounding up slaves—mostly boys between the ages of six and fifteen—whom they sent back to Constantinople.

Turkish slavery was different from other forms of slavery, however, such as that of African slaves in the New World. Except for the galley slaves on Turkish ships, most slaves were not required to perform cruel labors. For some, life was easier than their previous lives as serfs in eastern Europe had been. Ottoman slaves could enrich themselves, and those in the royal household often became powerful men, commanding armies and governing provinces of the empire. The female slaves who formed the sultan's harem were well treated, and their children respected. Almost every sultan was the son of a slave mother.

Controlling Trade

Constantinople controlled the strait between the Mediterranean and the Black Sea. The Ottomans levied duties on goods traded between Europe and the nations bordering the Black Sea, where they themselves soon acquired territory that allowed them to control the region's overland trade with northern Europe and Muscovy. The revenue went into expanding the Turkish navy, which soon asserted itself over the entire eastern Mediterranean, defeating the Venetians in the process. By the end of the fifteenth century, Mehmed's successors had pushed Ottoman power in Europe north to the Danube River, where they made peace with the Hungarians in 1484.

Decorative tiles at the Topkapi Palace in Istanbul show figs and grapes. Also known as the Seraglio, the palace was built by Mehmed II as an imposing royal center for the empire.

The Safavids and the Mamluks

The empire was increasingly hemmed in in the Islamic world. The Mamluks still ruled Egypt, and in the east the Safavids had risen to power in Iran (*see 3:397*). While the Ottomans followed the majority Sunni branch of Islam, the Safavids were Shiite Muslims. The new dynasty provided a focus for discontented Turkoman princes who resented centralized Ottoman control. When Mehmed II failed to react to the growing threat in the east, the Janissaries dethroned him in favor of his son, Selim I.

The coup showed how strong the Christian military elite had become. Selim hastened to establish his personal control over the army and, in 1514, routed the Safavids at Chaldiran inside the Iranian border. While Selim's army had cannons and gunpowder weapons, the Iranians fought with bows and arrows. Selim pulled back after his victory, but the Ottomans later permanently captured Mesopotamia, or present-day Iraq.

In the winter of 1516 and 1517, Selim turned against the Mamluks of Egypt. They

A detail from a fourteenth-century Ottoman manuscript shows a surgeon preparing to operate on a patient. The Ottomans were heirs to a long tradition of scholarship and learning in the Arab world, which also included classical Western sources, about subjects such as medicine, math, and geography.

105

The Middle East

What we know today as the Middle East was known by Europeans in the sixteenth and seventeenth centuries as the Levant. The name comes from the French word *lever*, meaning to rise, because the sun rises in the east. The Levant stretched around the eastern end of the Mediterranean from Asia Minor in the north to Egypt in the south and included what are today Syria, Jordan, Lebanon, and Israel.

Most of the population of the various Levantine countries was and remains Arabic, and the majority remains Islamic in its religion. An urban, materially rich Arab culture flourished in the region before the Ottoman conquest of the Mamluk empire in the sixteenth century brought a period of poverty and decline to the region's towns that lasted until the early twentieth century.

The Middle East has a long history. It was one of the cradles of civilization and was the home of three major religions: Judaism, Christianity, and Islam. In its geographical position, the region lies open to different influences. It forms a land bridge that connects Europe, Africa, and Asia and has long been a crossroads for population movements.

In the fifteenth and sixteenth centuries, the Levant thrived on trade with European powers, particularly Venice and Genoa. The region stood on important trade routes. Caravans south across the Sudan linked the region to sub-Saharan Africa. Other routes, such as the famed Silk Road, led across central Asia to reach India and China. Sea routes connected the coast with the trading ports of Greece, with the Italian peninsula, and beyond.

The walls around the Old City of Jerusalem were built by the Ottoman Turks, who conquered the city in the sixteenth century. The most symbolically important city in the Levant, Jerusalem was a holy place for both Christians and Muslims.

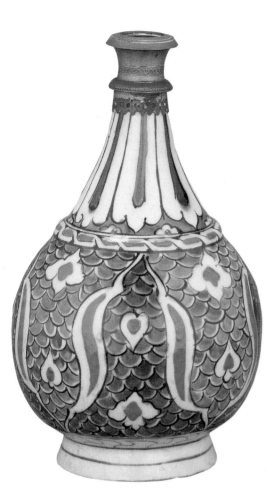

This sixteenth-century ceramic jug is in a style called Iznik ware, named for the town from which it came. Iznik ceramicists adapted colors and shapes from as far away as Ming China.

the peak of Ottoman power. The new sultan had more personal authority than any of his predecessors. He was richer, too: the conquest of the Arab world had doubled the revenues of the Ottoman treasury.

Süleyman was eager for expansion, but he faced a strong new power in Europe, the Habsburg Empire. Urged on by France, which wanted to limit Habsburg power, Süleyman crushed Hungary at the Battle of Mohacs (1526) and made it a vassal state. In 1529, he laid siege to the Austrian capital, Vienna, but his armies were too far from home to supply efficiently and were driven back. In 1536, Süleyman rewarded his French allies by giving the French the right to travel and trade in his dominions.

The outstanding Ottoman architect Sinan (1489–1588) built this mosque in Edirne, Turkey, in honor of the sultan Selim II.

were ripe for defeat. Mamluk power had been declining since Portuguese navigators discovered a sea route around Africa to India. The discovery made redundant the trade routes between Europe and the Far East that had been the source of Mamluk wealth. Selim won an easy victory. The Ottoman forces were better disciplined than their opponents, and many Mamluk officials betrayed their rulers in return for promises of important positions.

At a stroke, Selim's victory doubled the size of the empire, which now covered the major centers of the Islamic world except Safavid Iran and Mogul India. Mamluk territory contained the holy places of Islam, including Mecca, reinforcing the sultan's claim to spiritual authority. From the Arab world, Constantinople attracted Muslim intellectuals, scholars, and artists.

Süleyman the Magnificent

In 1520, Selim's son, Süleyman (c. 1494–1566), came to the throne. Known as the Lawgiver by the Ottomans and the Magnificent by Europeans, Süleyman ruled at

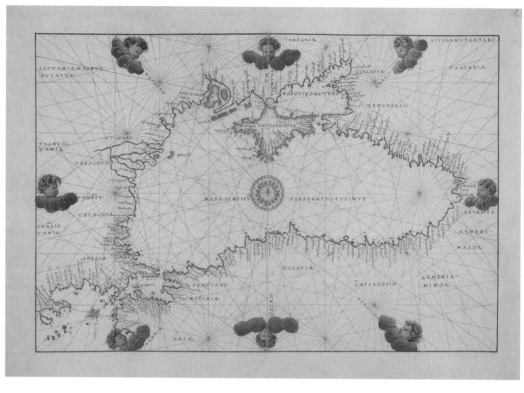

This vellum chart from 1544 shows direct lines for sailing between ports in the Black Sea. The sea provided a rich trading empire for the Ottomans, whose control of the strait that led to the Mediterranean—shown at bottom left of the map—enabled them to levy taxes on all shipping in the region.

The Ottomans built this fort in Nea Paphos, on the island of Cyprus, in 1592. They had captured the island only around twenty years earlier and built fortifications to defend it against a possible Christian assault.

Although his ambition was thwarted in Europe, Süleyman continued to strengthen Ottoman power in the Mediterranean. Despite opposition from a Habsburg navy, Süleyman's navy won the last Venetian possesssions in the Aegean in 1538. The sultan also made peace with the Safavids, securing the empire's eastern borders.

In 1571, the Turkish navy captured the Mediterranean island of Cyprus. In reply, a European alliance called the Holy League inflicted a massive naval defeat on the Turks, destroying virtually their entire fleet at Lepanto, off Greece.

It was a sign of Ottoman strength that the navy was quickly rebuilt and soon reestablished its dominance of the eastern Mediterranean. The empire remained strong: Ottoman power covered Cyprus, the Balkans, and Asia Minor, as well as the Middle East and most of North Africa.

At the start of the seventeenth century, Ottoman rule was at its height. At its height, however, the empire also contained the seeds of its decay. Expansion and success were weakening its internal structures. The Ottomans were about to enter a long period of decline (*see 6:727*).

Developments in Africa

The Rise and Fall of African Empires

For most of recorded history, Africa's geography effectively split the continent into two. The vast, sandy wastelands of the Sahara Desert and the scrub of the Sudan divide the coastal lands of the north from the mass of central and southern Africa, known as sub-Saharan Africa. The two regions followed distinct paths of development. North Africa belonged to the literate Mediterranean world. Its history was recorded first by the Egyptians, then the ancient Greeks and Romans, and later the Arabs. About sub-Saharan Africa, on the other hand, historians know relatively little

because its early nonliterate cultures left no written records. Scholars rely on archaeological and linguistic studies to piece together the early modern history of sub-Saharan Africa.

Ancient Roots
North Africa was a long-established center of settlement for peoples whose background linked them to the peoples of Europe and the Middle East. The Nile Valley had for thousands of years supported the civilization of ancient Egypt. West of the Nile Valley, in the less fertile lands that

This terracotta figure of a man seated behind a woman was buried in a grave in the Central African kingdom of Mali around 1400. Mali was a flourishing culture whose king Mansa Musa astonished the Arab world with his wealth.

109

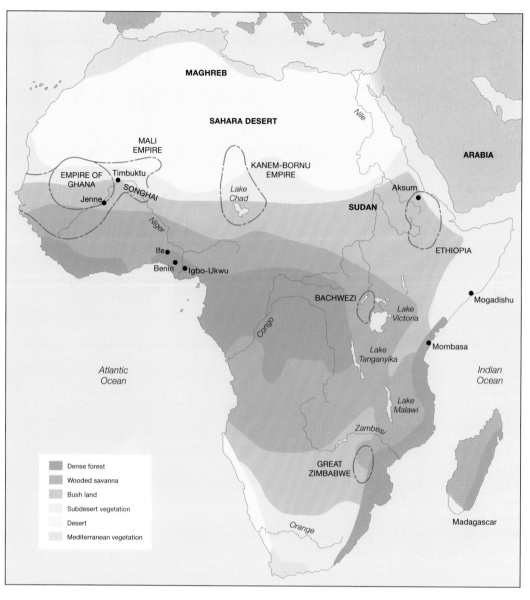

This map of Africa shows the various empires that grew up on the continent at various times between the tenth and fourteenth centuries and Africa's different ecological zones as they exist today.

stretched from Libya to Morocco, life for the Berber people remained chiefly nomadic, a term that derives from the Latin for "wanderer."

The empires of Greece and Rome built cities along the North African coasts without establishing territorial control, although the Romans introduced Christianity to the region. In the seventh century, Arab Muslims took control first of Egypt and then of the Maghreb, the coastal lands of the western Mediterranean. Islam replaced Christianity as the religion of most North Africans. In the sixteenth century, the Maghreb fell under the sway of the Turkish Ottoman Empire (*see 1:107*).

Sub-Saharan Africa

Sub-Saharan Africa is sometimes also referred to as black Africa because the majority of its inhabitants are black Africans. This part of the continent is also home to hunter-gatherer peoples, however, such as the Khoisan, who belong to a dif-

ferent human grouping and, on the island of Madagascar off the east coast, descendants of Indonesian settlers (*see 3:315*). Black Africans themselves include many different peoples, each of whom has different ways of life, different religions, and different forms of government. Most of them speak different languages, which linguists group into larger families that suggest links between groups.

In the early modern period, some tribal groups lived in small communities in wood-and-mud huts while others lived in stone dwellings in great trading cities. The majority of black Africans, however, were farmers or herders, though the tsetse fly made it difficult to raise cattle in western parts of the continent. Farmers tilled the fields with wooden hoes and grew sorghum and pearl millet as their basic cereals; in west Africa, the wet climate encouraged the growing of African yams, oil palm, and kola nuts. By the fifteenth century, Africans were also growing crops that originated in

A caravan of camels crosses the desert in present-day Algeria. Vast trains of camels carried gold, ivory, and salt north across the Sahara and Sudan to northern Africa. The most significant commodity to cross the desert, however, was African slaves bound for the Islamic world. Such slaves were often prisoners from wars between African kingdoms.

Southeast Asia, including bananas and Asian rice. Although historians do not know how such crops came to Africa, some suggest that their arrival is connected with the Indonesian settlers of Madagascar.

Africa's Geography

The range of lifestyles in sub-Saharan Africa reflects the continent's varied geography. South of the Sahara Desert lie a band of scrub and the grasslands of the Sudanese savanna. On the coast of West Africa and in the basin of the Congo River stand extensive rain forests at the edge of which wooded savanna extends east and south into a region of brush bounded by desert to the west and forests in the east.

The majority of black Africans speak Bantu languages, although Bantu speakers include numerous ethnic groups. Historians believe that the Bantu originated in the savanna of West Africa before beginning to migrate east and south around 3000 B.C.E. The Bantu brought cattle and wet-climate crops and adopted millet and sorghum from the peoples they encountered. The success of Bantu agriculture led to the displacement of the indigenous hunter-gatherers.

This aerial photograph shows the Niger River of West Africa. The great rivers of the continent—the Nile in the northeast, the Niger and Congo in the center, and the Zambesi and Orange in the south—were of limited use in trade because of rapids and waterfalls.

This brass statue from the sixteenth century shows Idia, the mother of the king of Benin. Idia used her mystical powers to help Benin in a war against its neighbors, and heads such as this one were set up on altars as a reward. Like other Islamicized African states, Benin maintained strong links with traditional folk culture.

Barriers and Trade

Many parts of Africa are relatively isolated by mountain ranges or deep valleys. Thick forests, arid deserts, and rapids and waterfalls on the rivers make communication difficult. Such barriers are not impenetrable, however. Mediterranean travelers crossed the Sahara Desert from classical times on. When the Arabs arrived, they continued trading across the deserts with West Africa via well-established caravan routes. The sub-Sahara supplied gold, ivory, and slaves. In return, the Arabs brought luxury goods, horses, and salt. Salt was in short supply in much of Africa but was essential for living and for seasoning the cereal-based diet. Where people had no access to salt mines or lakes and imported salt was too expensive, they burned marsh plants and used their ash as a substitute.

The Muslim traders discovered a sub-Saharan culture with thriving internal trade and great cities, ruled by kings whose subjects revered them as gods. Among the states the Arabs encountered was Kanem-Bornu, which lay north and east of Lake Chad, at the hub of trade routes between North Africa, the Nile Valley, and sub-Saharan Africa. Founded in the ninth century by the Sef dynasty, Kanem flourished on trade and on rich agriculture. Its people raised goats, cattle, camels, and horses; they planted millet, beans, and wheat.

Ghana

Of the early kingdoms the Arabs encountered, the most powerful was Ghana, which lay about 500 miles north and west of the modern country of the same name. Ghana grew rich on the export of gold to North Africa and from there to the whole Islamic world; the Arabs called it "the land of gold." In the tenth century, an Arab traveler reported seeing a merchant make out an order for 20,000 gold sovereigns to be paid to a trader in Morocco. Another traveler reported that the king of Ghana raised taxes on the salt and copper entering or leaving his kingdom.

The king's taxes went toward supporting a powerful court within his walled palace. Next to the mud-built capital city stood a stone town built by Muslim traders. Ghana declined in the eleventh century under pressure from the Muslim Almoravids, Berber nomads from the north.

Islam and East Africa

The emergence of the Almoravids had a profound influence. From contact with North Africa, they had adopted a militant form of Islam. As they rose to domination, the ruling and merchant classes of the Sudan also began to convert to Islam. They had traded with the Islamic world for centuries and perhaps saw an economic advantage in conversion. African kings, however, also continued to claim the blessing of local gods, because they needed to keep the support of the local population.

Islam also had a profound effect on Africa's east coast. For centuries the coast had been linked to maritime trade networks that extended north to Arabia and east to the islands of the Indian Ocean, to India itself, and beyond. By the tenth century, ivory from Africa was reaching China, and Chinese porcelain arrived in towns such as Kilwa, Mogadishu, and Mombasa.

The Arab intermediaries of this trade, who came mainly from the Persian Gulf, built Muslim cities on islands just off the coast of the mainland. They also colonized African cities, mixing with Africans to produce a mixed-race Muslim ruling class that dominated the largely independent city-states of the coast. They built homes and mosques of stone and coral and used strings of seashells such as blue and red cowries to serve as money. Cowries from the islands of the Indian Ocean were also used as currency in parts of India and China, enabling international trade.

Skill in Sculpting

The emergence of centralized empires in West Africa encouraged the development of centers of power in neighboring areas. African traders hired local warriors to protect their trade caravans. Ambitious chiefs along the trade routes began to assume increased centralized power in order to maximize their natural resources.

Near the forested coast of West Africa, Benin and Yoruba, which is in modern Nigeria, supported highly developed urbanized cultures by around the twelfth century. Both cultures are renowned for their sculptors, who produced naturalistic brass and bronze figures. They used the lost-wax process, in which figures were constructed around a wax mold that was then melted away.

Such achievements in metalworking confirm that metallurgy has a long history in Africa. The Bantu acquired techniques

Cowrie shells surround a face carved in bone in this display from modern-day Africa. Cowries and other seashells were a valuable form of currency along the East African coast.

for making iron around 3,000 years ago, around the same time as Europeans and peoples of the Middle East. For many years, European historians assumed that knowledge of metallurgy spread to black Africa from the Near East and North Africa. Now, however, some claim that the differences in smelting techniques between sub-Saharan Africa and the Mediterranean world suggest that black Africans may have developed their knowledge of metallurgy independently. Knowledge of how to build furnaces and bellows spread into the continent from the plateau of Nigeria and from the Nile Valley. The importance of metalworking is suggested by the fact that blacksmiths acquired a prominent status and political power in many communities.

A dhow sails into a harbor on the island of Zanzibar. Zanzibar's ideal position for trade with the African interior attracted settlers from Iran as early as the tenth century. The Iranians were absorbed into the local population, many of whose members still call themselves Shirazi, after Shiraz, the region from which most of the Iranians came. Later, Arab merchants made Zanzibar a major trading station and became the island's aristocracy until the arrival of the Portuguese in the sixteenth century.

113

This shrine stands in Kaba Kangaba, which was the capital of the Malinke kingdom that became the empire of Mali. First built around the thirteenth century, the shrine has been rebuilt every seven years since. It honors the Keita clan, who claim as their ancestor Sundiata, the founder of Mali.

Instruments of Exchange

One of the most important metals, particularly in central Africa, was copper, which was used to make jewelry and ornaments. Copper also made the musical instruments that accompanied local rulers as they toured their domains. The development of centralized political authority in parts of the continent prompted an increased demand for copper to create court regalia.

In what is now Zaire, one of the world's great sources of copper, standard ingots were cast for trade. Such ingots made their way north across the Sahara. After contact with the Dutch in the sixteenth century, miners on the Congo River exchanged copper for Chinese porcelain, South American tobacco, and Indian textiles.

Textiles were an important form of exchange in much of Africa. In western central Africa, they were made from fiber from the raffia plant, which was an important source of trading power for the Kongo kingdom. The finished cloth had a velvet texture and came in a range of natural colors. Cloth was an important possession among peoples who did not have much gold or cattle, the traditional sources of status in many African societies. It was given in return for a wife, for example. Old men controlled the cloth trade, enabling them to buy numerous younger wives.

African trade was so extensive that people used many means of exchange. Rock salt, cotton cloth, and copper bracelets were used as money in various parts of the continent. Horses, which were rare in Africa, were highly valued. A Moroccan horse was reckoned to be worth twelve slaves in about 1500. In central Africa, people traded dried fish, which was valu-

These fish are drying in the sun in modern Africa. In central Africa, dried fish were an important source of wealth for communities with access to the region's many lakes.

able because other foods soon perished in the heat. Porters carried bundles of dried fish on their heads along long routes to trade with people who needed a reliable source of protein.

Great Zimbabwe

To the south, beyond the influence of Islam, a trading empire grew up whose chief record is the site of Great Zimbabwe, near Nyanda in Zimbabwe. The site is the largest of many stone ruins in what are now Zimbabwe and Mozambique. The name Zimbabwe itself is Bantu for "stone dwelling." While most of Africa's peoples built enclosures of wood and reeds, the Karanga people who lived on the site of Great Zimbabwe from the eleventh to the fifteenth centuries built a vast royal or religious complex of stone buildings and defenses. Without using mortar, Karanga builders constructed walls and towers that still remain standing. They smelted gold, which they traded with Arab intermediaries on the coast of the Indian Ocean for glass beads and porcelain from China.

The Emergence of Mali

In western Africa, the Islamic kingdom of Mali emerged from the ashes of Ghana in the middle of the thirteenth century. As Ghana declined, due largely to the interruption of its trade by the Almoravids, the mantle of leadership in the region passed to the Mandinka people of the upper Niger Valley. The Mandinka had come into only limited contact with Islam before their rise to prominence under the great warrior-chieftain Sundiata (d. 1255). Sundiata was a pagan, but he and his successors converted to Islam, probably because they believed it would bring them political and economic advantages.

Adherence to the Islamic faith established a basis of cooperation between Mali merchants and the Islamic kingdoms of north Africa. Islam also provided a useful bond between the various tribes that lived within the Mali kingdom, submerging their tribal loyalties in a greater loyalty to the ruling dynasty.

Mansa Musa

During the thirteenth and fourteenth centuries, the Mandinka rulers of Mali came to dominate West African trade. By the time the most famous of all African chieftains, Mansa Musa (d. 1332?), came to the throne in 1307, Mali was a vast empire that stretched nearly 1,000 miles from the Atlantic coast to the borders of modern Nigeria and from the Sahara to the edge of the tropical forest belt. Its power was attested by the number of vassal states that it was able to bring under its sway, most notably the kingdom of Songhai on the middle Niger. Songhai, which itself had adopted Islam in the eleventh century, ran a

Trees rise above the wall of the so-called royal enclosure at Great Zimbabwe. The wall surrounds an elliptical enclosure whose exact purpose is not known. It was possibly home to a royal palace or to ceremonial religious buildings.

The Bantu Migration

Historians of early Africa face a number of problems. The most serious is the lack of written records. No early sub-Saharan African civilization was literate. The first documentary evidence about that part of the continent comes from Arabs who arrived around the tenth century. Scholars of African prehistory piece together the continent's past not only from physical evidence such as archaeological sites and artifacts but also from the evidence of Africa's many languages.

Africa is home to a remarkable 1,500 different languages, which linguists group into five major families. One-quarter of all the world's languages are spoken only in Africa. The distribution of languages throughout the continent and differences and similarities among language families provide vital clues about the prehistoric movement and interaction of the peoples who speak them. They suggest that the distribution of Africa's peoples was once very different from what it is today.

The peoples of North Africa speak mainly Afroasiatic languages related to the Semitic languages of the Middle East. South of the Sahara occurs a language family called Nilo-Saharan. Most of sub-Saharan Africa is dominated by a large language family called Niger-Congo. There are other languages, however, spoken mainly by relatively primitive hunter-gathering peoples. Some speak languages called Khoisan, which are full of distinctive clicks that linguists denote by an exclamation mark, as in the name of the !Kung people.

The inhabitants of the island of Madagascar, just 250 miles off the east African coast, speak an Austronesian language related to those spoken in the Pacific region. The island is peopled by a mixture of black Africans and Southeast Asians from Borneo in Indonesia, over 4,000 miles away across the Indian Ocean. In one of the great migrations of human history, the prehistoric Indonesians navigated the open sea, bringing their Austronesian culture to Africa. U.S. physiologist Jared Diamond calls this "the most astonishing fact of human geography for the entire world."

The dominant languages throughout the southern third of Africa belong to Bantu, a subfamily of the Niger-Congo family. The term *Bantu* is also used to refer to the peoples who speak Bantu languages, although such peoples are ethnically varied. More than 200 million Africans speak about 500 variations of Bantu, which are so similar that they have been described as dialects of a single language.

Bantu peoples already dominated southern Africa by the time written records began. Linguistic evidence, however, reveals that this was not always the case. In particular, some Khoisan speakers are isolated today. Two groups live in modern Tanzania, separated by over 1,000 miles from the center of Khoisan languages in southern Africa. Such a distribution suggests that the Khoisan were once widespread throughout the region until they were displaced by Bantu speakers. Other hunter-gatherer peoples such as the Mbuti, Aka, and Twa adopted the languages of the Bantu newcomers, who were farmers and cattle herders, keeping

This metal figure, made to commemorate a dead person by the Kota of Gabon in central Africa, testifies to the ironworking skills of the Bantu-speaking peoples.

A young African boy stands guard ready to scare crows from a field of sorghum in Ethiopia. Like millet, sorghum was one of the crops that enabled the Bantu migration.

only a few words and sounds from their original languages.

Where did the Bantu originate? Why did they spread so widely and how did they so successfully displace the region's indigenous inhabitants? Linguistics provides part of the answer. The Bantu languages are closely related, suggesting that the dispersal of their speakers happened long enough ago to allow languages to evolve but recently enough for them to remain closely related. Linguists reckon this process to have begun around 5,000 years ago. The most distinctive Bantu languages occur in the rain forests of modern Cameroon and Nigeria, in west central Africa, suggesting that this is where the Bantu-speaking peoples originated. Around 3,000 B.C.E., the Bantu began to migrate south and east from their homeland, probably in response to population pressure.

Words common in all Bantu languages suggest that, by the time the migration began, the Bantu were already raising cattle and growing wet-climate crops such as yams, though they still also relied on hunting and gathering for food. In East Africa, where their wet-climate crops flourished, the Bantu encountered Nilo-Saharan farmers from whom they learned to grow millet and sorghum. Bantu speakers reached the East African coast by the last centuries B.C.E. and there came into contact with Austronesians from Madagascar, from whom they adopted important food crops such as the Asian yam and the banana.

About 1000 B.C.E., the Bantu developed ironworking. At a similar date, ironworking from the Middle East was adopted in North Africa. Historians once believed that ironworking was carried across the Sahara Desert to the rest of Africa. More recent studies highlight the different ironworking techniques of northern and southern Africa. They suggest that sub-Saharan peoples developed ironworking independently, drawing on a heritage of copper smelting that was already 1,000 years old.

The combination of wet-climate crops and iron tools and weapons gave the Bantu a telling edge over the indigenous peoples with whom they were competing. Some hunter-gatherers withdrew into the equatorial forests. Others, particularly the Khoi and the San, moved south before the advancing Bantu.

The Bantu expansion stopped at the Fish River, however, east of modern Cape Town. Their crops needed summer rain and would not grow in the wet winters of the south. The consequence of this botanical detail was profound. When Dutch settlers arrived in southern Africa in 1652, the cape was sparsely occupied by Khoi and San whom Europeans could easily overrun. Had they encountered steel-equipped Bantu farmers, the history of European settlement might have been far different.

In a scene unchanged for centuries, bowls called calabashes await sale at a market at Mopti, on the Niger River. Mopti was a depot for Saharan trade caravans. A similar beneficial location supported the great empires of Songhai and Mali.

This straw enclosure was built by San inhabitants who live in reserves in South Africa. Early encounters with hunter-gatherer peoples such as the San and the Khoi encouraged Europeans' superior attitude toward Africans.

flourishing trading kingdom from its major cities, Gao and Timbuktu.

In 1324, Mansa Musa made an historic pilgrimage to Mecca. An immensely rich man, he was said to have as many as 10,000 horses in his stables. His journey to Mecca, accompanied by a vast retinue of richly clothed servants, caused a sensation. So much gold did he carry that, when he reached Cairo, it caused a decline in the value of the local currency.

Mansa Musa brought sub-Saharan Africa to the attention of much of the Mediterranean world for the first time. In 1375, Mali took center stage in the first European map of West Africa. Mansa Musa returned from Mecca with architects who introduced brick-building and with scholars who made the cities of Timbuktu and Jenne into centers of Islamic law and theology.

The European View

Despite the wealth of Mansa Musa or the achievements of Great Zimbabwe, the first Europeans to come into contact with Africa reported its poverty and backwardness. One wrote: "They have no shirts; they envelop their bodies above their pants with a bit of material… most of them go bareheaded and barefoot." Another recorded that they lived in round huts without furniture or windows and mocked the habit of filling houses with smoke in order to keep away biting gnats. He wrote: "Not everyone is accustomed as they are to be smoked like hams and to be smitten with a smell of smoke which makes people sick."

Such dismissive views of Africa's cultures laid the foundation for Europe's later colonization of the continent (*see 6:817*). Europe's attitudes were ill founded on the eve of its invasion that brought the age of firearms and an expanded slave trade to Africa. The continent was home to myriad cultures vastly different from Europe's. In Ethiopia, Egyptian influence from the Nile Valley had led to the creation of a literate, Christian society. Europeans were prepared to acknowledge few similarities between themselves and black Africans, however. Unknown to them and barely appreciated even by the neighboring Islamic world, southern, central, and northern Africa had long been home to numerous great empires and civilizations.

Developments in Asia

The Civilizations of China, Japan, and India

In 1271, one of the most famous travelers in history, the Venetian merchant Marco Polo (1254–1324), set out with his father and uncle on an overland journey to Beijing in China. There he entered the court of the mighty Mongol emperor Kublai Khan (1215–1294), whom he served as an ambassador and commercial agent for seventeen years, traveling widely through China.

Polo was not the first westerner to reach China; other traders and missionaries had been there before him, including his own father and uncle in the 1260s. What made Marco Polo's journey different was that, after he returned to Italy in 1295, he pub-

lished a long account of his experiences. He described the wonderful inventions that he found in China, and he heaped praise on the country for its wealth and expertise in manufacturing. Polo even described the city of Hangzhou, with its more than one million residents, as "the finest and noblest city in the world." The book's rare glimpse of distant Asia made it instantly popular. It confirmed the European view of East Asia—known then as Cathay—as a place of luxury, splendor, and mystery.

The European view of Asia, in general, was of a land of exotic silks and spices. The lure of Asian riches propelled all the early European explorers, who sought to find a

The Great Wall of China was built in the second century B.C.E. to protect the Chinese from foreign invasion. Despite such a formidable defense, China has fallen under foreign rule numerous times throughout its history.

119

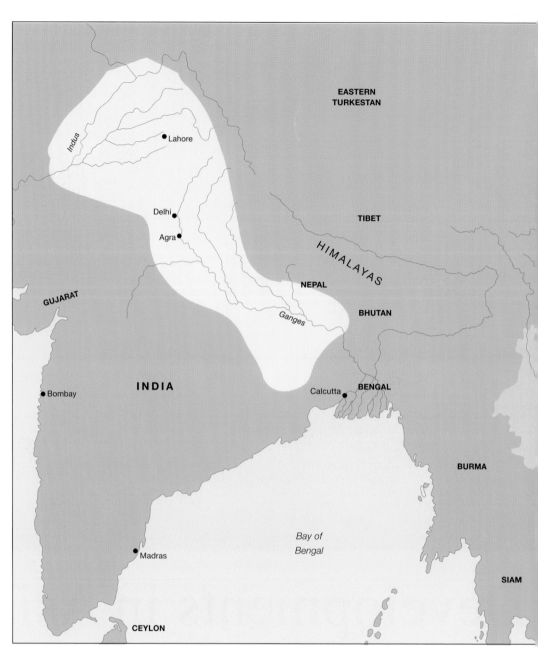

This map shows the two dominant empires of Asia—Mogul India and Ming China—in the latter half of the sixteenth century.

sea route to the East (*see 3:298*). Yet, for many centuries after Polo's journey, East and West remained largely ignorant of each other. Even toward the end of the Middle Ages, Europe was still too isolated to establish contacts much beyond its borders. China, by contrast, was near the peak of its splendor and neither wanted, nor required, anything from the West.

The Rise of China's Sung Dynasty

The history of China from the second half of the tenth century is the story of the gradual spread of centralized imperial control over the whole country. The same process of the centralization of power occurred later, and much less successfully, in neighboring Japan and India, where local rulers retained considerable amounts of power. In the early modern period, a similar emergence of centralized power and state for-

mation would change the political shape of Europe (*see 1:19*).

The foundations of a unified Chinese state were laid by the emperors of the Sung dynasty, which began in 960. In that year, a northern warlord called Chao K'uang-yin (927–976) gave himself the name T'ai Tsu, and declared himself the first Sung emperor. At the time, China was divided into several quarreling states. T'ai Tsu brought the rival states under his rule, creating peace and stability. He deprived local warlords of their power and brought their private armies under imperial command. By the time he died in 976, T'ai Tsu had united all of China under imperial administration, almost as far north as the Great Wall. This great structure remained in the hands of two powerful groups: the Qidan of Liao in the northeast and the Tibetan state of Xia in the northwest.

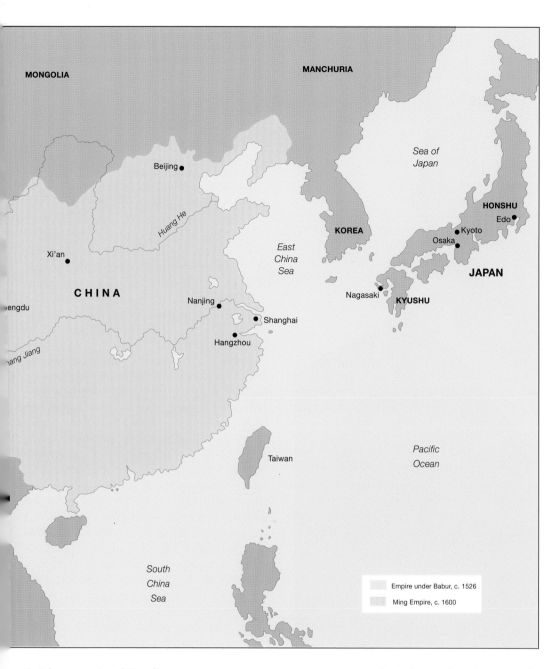

MONGOLIA

MANCHURIA

Sea of
Japan

HONSHU
Edo

Beijing

Huang He

KOREA

East
China
Sea

Kyoto
Osaka

JAPAN

Xi'an

CHINA

engdu

Nanjing

Nagasaki

KYUSHU

Shanghai

Hangzhou

ang Jiang

Pacific
Ocean

Taiwan

South
China
Sea

Empire under Babur, c. 1526

Ming Empire, c. 1600

Achievements of the Sung

The Sung era was notable for the steady development of technical expertise and the flourishing of artistic talent. Gunpowder, known in China from early times but used mainly for fireworks, was first used in weapons against marauders. Significant advances in medicine and biology were matched by an expanding economy. The output of silver and iron soared, creating a great rise in the production of handicrafts, which in turn led to the rapid growth of cities, including five with more than a million inhabitants.

The Sung introduced paper currency for the first time anywhere in the world. Large water irrigation schemes enabled peasants to increase their production of rice and feed the country's growing population. Improved methods of navigation and the construction of larger and more seaworthy ships supported the first real seaborne trade in Chinese history.

All these achievements far outpaced developments in Europe at that time. The Sung also brought about an artistic renaissance. Although most printing was done using carved wooden blocks, the introduction of a form of movable type led to a great increase in the publishing of classical Chinese texts. Pottery making, especially in green porcelain, was of an excellence not seen since the Han dynasty a thousand years earlier. Landscape painting—done in ink and watercolors on silk or paper—reached a peak that many Chinese experts believe has never been surpassed. It was in this period, too, that artists first combined painting and calligraphy—or artistic handwriting—in the same work. This combination would become a general characteristic of

This painting from about 1280 shows Chao Kou, the first emperor of the Southern Sung dynasty. Kou built a strong empire with a centralized bureaucracy and an efficient tax system.

Chinese art. Like other artistic developments under the Sung, it created an enduring legacy for future generations.

Threats from the North

Chinese rulers throughout history have feared central Asian marauders from the north and west. Such fears had prompted the building of the Great Wall in the second century B.C.E. From the tenth century, the Sung felt the pressure of the Qidan people of Liao, who dominated Manchuria, Mongolia, and much of northeast China. The Sung emperors paid the Qidan an annual tribute of silver and silk in an attempt to keep them peaceful.

It was not from the Qidan that the real threat eventually came, however. Early in the twelfth century, a warlike nomadic tribe called the Juchen, who were vassals of the Qidan, rose in revolt. In 1114, Akuta (1069–1163), the leader of the Juchen, declared the independence of his people and proclaimed himself emperor. The Sung, seeing what they thought was an opportunity to contain the Qidan, allied with the Juchen. It was a fatal mistake. The Juchen, who were militarily superior to both the Qidan and the Sung, swept southward. They overran Liao and in 1126 they captured the Sung capital of Kaifeng, taking prisoner the emperor and his court. They also carried off the imperial treasure.

The remnants of the Sung government retreated south and regrouped at Hangzhou. There they set up a new dynasty under the emperor's son, Chao Kou. This has become known as the Southern Sung dynasty, to distinguish it from the earlier empire of the Northern Sung.

In 1141, Chao Kou made peace with the Juchen. He accepted the status of vassal, executed his best general, and agreed to pay an annual tribute of silver and silk. The border between the two empires was confirmed as a line along the Huai and Wei Rivers, which cut China roughly in half.

The Arrival of the Mongols

For the rest of the twelfth century, the Sung prospered. A new threat was gathering in the steppe lands north of the Gobi Desert,

These ornate silver and gold boots were made in the Qidan kingdom of Liao in the century preceding its defeat by the Juchen in 1126.

however, in the shape of the fierce warrior nomads, the Mongols. Under their leader, Genghis Khan (1162–1227), Mongol horsemen set about carving out for themselves the biggest land empire the world has ever known.

Genghis, the son of a tribal chieftain, was the first leader to unite all the Mongol tribes by waging incessant warfare against those who opposed him. In 1206, he proclaimed himself the supreme leader, or khan, of all the Mongols. He then turned outward. In 1213, he led his armies across the Great Wall of China; within two years, he had devastated vast tracts of the Juchen empire. In 1218, he turned west, overrunning Turkestan, sacking the central Asian cities of Samarkand and Bokhara, cutting a swathe through Iran, and then sweeping north through the Caucasus into southern Russia. At his death, Genghis had laid the foundations of the great Mongol empire—stretching over China, India, central Asia, and parts of eastern Europe—that his successors built in the century after his death.

A Destroyer

Genghis was not interested in establishing settled rule of his conquests. He was interested in plunder; his armies left a trail of ruin and death in their wake. "Happiness," Genghis said, "lies in conquering one's enemies, in driving them in front of oneself, in taking their property, in savoring their despair, in outraging their wives and daughters." Cruelty was second nature to him and genocide a passion. Historians believe that when they captured one Juchen province, the Mongols killed 98 percent of its inhabitants.

Genghis did not conquer China himself. That task fell to his son, Ogedei, who defeated the Juchen in 1234 and set up Mongol rule over northern China. The Southern Sung continued to resist. In 1260, the Mongols hailed a new leader, Kublai Khan, grandson of Genghis, who was determined to rule over all of China. He achieved this in 1279, with victory in a final sea battle off what is now Hong Kong. To mark his success, Kublai announced the start of a new dynasty, called Yuan, which means "origin," indicating his intention to bring a fresh beginning to China.

China's Yuan Dynasty

For the first time, all of China was under foreign rule. Kublai was not just a soldier, like his grandfather, however; he was also a nation builder. He established his capital at Beijing, encouraged the arts, scholarship, and the Buddhist religion, and formed

This Sung dynasty illustration is part of a work painted on a long scroll of silk entitled *Going Upriver at the Ming Festival*. It gives a good impression of the busy trade in a provincial Chinese town in the early twelfth century.

This contemporary portrait shows Yorimoto Minamoto, who became the first shogun of Japan when his family overcame the Taira to establish their own power base in the islands.

trade links with other parts of Asia, the Middle East, and even Europe.

The Mongol invaders also achieved what no previous Chinese dynasty had been able to do: they created a unified China that has endured to the present day. Although unification was achieved by foreign invaders, however, the Mongols were content to adopt ancient Chinese patterns of government. As a nomadic people lacking developed systems of government of their own, they ruled in cooperation with local officials. China's own government lay in the hands of an aristocracy trained in the teachings of Confucianism. This system of ethical beliefs, originally developed by K'ung Ch'iu, known in the West as Confucius (551–479 B.C.E.), created a tradition of nobles trained in a humanistic view of government. Positions in China's government were awarded to intellectuals who passed examinations in Confucianism, creating a bureaucracy that depended on ability rather than birth.

A statue of a tortoise marks the site of Karakorum in Mongolia, once the capital of Genghis Khan's Mongol empire. The stupas in the background are part of a later Buddhist monastery on the site.

This carved wooden figure from the fifteenth or sixteenth century shows a Japanese Zen monk. Zen was a Japanese sect of Buddhism, which originally came to Japan from China. It stressed the importance of meditation as a means of achieving enlightenment.

A Chinese scholar named Hsü Heng (1290–1281) introduced Kublai's court to Confucianism and began to educate the sons of the Mongol nobility to become teachers of the discipline themselves. So deeply did the Mongols absorb Chinese influences that the idea of a separate Mongol identity gradually began to disappear. Mongol China became Chinese.

The Mongols were not successful in all their military efforts. An attempt to subdue Southeast Asia failed because of the resistance of the Vietnamese. Expeditions against Japan ended in disaster. In 1281, the weather saved Japan from a Mongol invasion force of 140,000 soldiers. At a critical moment, a typhoon, called in Japanese *kamikaze*, or "divine wind," blew up and sank the Mongol fleet.

Developments in Japan

From very early times, the warrior tradition had been strong in the islands of Japan. Constant wars between the great families, or clans, led to a feud in the twelfth century between the houses of Minamoto and Taira. In 1185, the Minamoto emerged victorious under their leader, Yorimoto (1147–1199), who declared himself the nation's first shogun, meaning "great military comman-

This garden of rock and sand stands near a Buddhist temple in Japan. Such gardens are built as an aid to meditation; their elements are symbols of the natural landscape.

der and ruler." This victory marked a watershed in Japan's history and began a new age, the Kamakura shogunate. The shogunate was a military dictatorship that coexisted with Japan's imperial dynasty.

Before the Kamakura era, Japan had been increasingly influenced by many aspects of Chinese culture. In the early Middle Ages, Japanese emperors had tried to introduce a Chinese style of government, with an

Himeji Castle rises above its defensive foundations in Hyogo, Japan. Such well-defended castles served as the bases for the warlords of the clans, which continually fought one another or the central government.

administration of elite officials appointed by the central state to obtain taxes and labor from the population. Chinese writing and Buddhism also made their way across the sea to Japan.

Chinese models of government were not suitable in Japan, however. The great land-owning families retained too much power and had private armies of knights, called samurai. Warfare was endemic as clans fought one another to establish dominance and fought to resist the power of the emperor and his government. As long as the clans remained at war with each other, they could not seriously threaten the emperor's position. This situation changed when the Minamoto emerged as the most powerful clan in Japan.

In some ways, Japan resembled the feudal states of medieval Europe. Although Japan had its own monarch in the form of the emperor, he had no real power. The Minamoto shogun, Yorimoto, simply ignored the imperial court at Kyoto and set up a rival government at Kamakura. Although the emperor continued to rule in name from Kyoto, real power in Japan was wielded by the Kamakura shogunate. This division of power would continue until the nineteenth century.

The Ashikaga Shogunate

The Kamakura shogunate lasted until 1336, when it was defeated by the Ashikaga clan. The Ashikaga shogunate, though it was to last until 1573, never established firm control over the whole of Japan. The Ashikaga period was marked by periodic clan warfare and political disorder. It was, however, an era of great cultural achievement.

The Ashikaga shoguns sought prestige from missions to China, and the contact between the two countries revived Chinese influence in Japan. Zen Buddhist monks drew on Chinese inspiration to become leading scholars at the court, while artists soon rivaled the landscape painters of China. Architects created the magnificent Golden and Silver Pavilions at Kyoto and became expert at laying out landscape gardens at monasteries and palaces.

China's Ming Dynasty

Much of the cultural activity in Japan was a reflection of the high culture of Ming China. In the mid–fourteenth century, a rash of peasant revolts brought down the Yuan dynasty, which gave way, in 1368, to a purely Chinese dynasty, the Ming. Under the Ming, China expanded to take in its southern neighbors, Annam and Siam, now called Vietnam and Thailand, respectively.

The Ming also sent out trading missions that established links as far away as Sri Lanka, the Persian Gulf, and East Africa.

In 1433, however, the Ming suddenly ceased its overseas activity in what is known as the Great Withdrawal. The emperor forbade his subjects to go abroad. By 1500, it was punishable by death to build a ship with more than two masts, limiting all sailors to China's coastal waters. Partly, the withdrawal was economic. It was expensive for the Ming to impress their trading partners with China's material accomplishments. The funds spent on sending treasures abroad could more usefully be used to build granaries and canals or to strengthen the Great Wall.

The withdrawal also owed something to China's view of itself. The Chinese—who sometimes called themselves the Sons of Heaven and believed that China lay at the center of the universe—believed that they had little benefit to gain from contact with what they saw as barbarian nations. Confucianism encouraged their inward emphasis, arguing that the physical shape of the world was unimportant compared

This porcelain jar dates from the Ming dynasty of the early fifteenth century in China. Ming porcelain was in great demand in the world. It served as a model for Ottoman potters in Turkey, for example, and remains of Chinese pottery have also been found in eastern Africa.

Stern but wise, the face of a Ming emperor or one of his retainers stares out from a tomb built in Beijing during the sixteenth century.

This watchtower rises above the imperial palace in Beijing. The Ming dynasty greatly enhanced the vast imperial and administrative center called the Forbidden City in the heart of the Chinese capital.

the Imperial Palace complex in Beijing and the great carved tombs of the emperors. As long as the Chinese still traded overseas, Ming porcelain was in great demand, as were lacquerwork and carved jade. Perhaps the most famous artists of the Ming era were the painters of the Wu School, headed by Shen Zhou, the first Chinese painter to incorporate his own poetry into his paintings and one of the first to include human figures in his landscapes.

The Ching Dynasty

The Ming emperors, like all those before them, always kept a nervous eye on their northern frontiers. To protect themselves, they repaired gaps in the Great Wall and fortified many of the northern towns. In spite of all their precautions, they found themselves impotent against a new wave of "barbarian" invasions from the north, this time from a branch of the Juchen tribes called the Manchu.

The end of the Ming dynasty was a sorry affair. In 1618, the Manchu had overrun the northeast province of Liaodong, seizing it from the Ming and creating their capital at Mukden, now known as Shenyang. In 1644, a Chinese rebel called Li Zicheng captured the Ming capital of Beijing, at which point a Ming army commander in the north called in the Manchu to help him to defeat the rebel. The Manchu armies

with the internal world of the spirit. While European sailors were exploring the globe—the first Europeans arrived at the Ming court in 1514—the Chinese entered a long period of isolation.

In China itself, some of the Ming dynasty's most notable achievements were ambitious architectural projects, including

جا رحد این چشمه به سیا فی که نیا ختی شد در و قت ثشکفتن کل ار غوان این قمربا

معلو م نیست که در عالم بو ده با شدار غوان زرد او هم بسیا رمیثو دار غوان زردوا رغوا

This contemporary painting shows Babur, founder of the Mogul dynasty, visiting a spring at Kabul, in modern Afghanistan. The painting is done in an Iranian style, reflecting Babur's foreign origins and Islamic faith.

crossed the Great Wall into China, where they drove Li Zicheng to flight. When the Ming set off in pursuit of the rebel, the Manchu spread through northern China. They entered Beijing and installed their own king as the first Ching emperor (*see* *4:523*). The last Ming emperor hanged himself in the palace garden.

The Rise of Muslim India

The only Asian civilization to rival China in its wealth and achievements from the fifteenth to seventeenth centuries was that of India. In the late twelfth century, Afghan Muslims invaded north India and overran the plains of the Ganges River. In 1206, a Muslim general declared himself sultan of

129

Delhi, marking the beginning of Muslim rule over northern India. The Delhi sultanate never succeeded in bringing all of India under its sway. That work of unification was left to the Moguls.

The Mogul Empire

The founder of the Mogul empire was Babur (1483–1530), a Turk from central Asia who claimed descent from both the Turkic warrior Timur and the Mongol Genghis Khan. The name of the Mogul dynasty comes from the Hindu word for Mongol. Aged only eighteen, Babur took control of the oasis city of Samarkand in modern Uzbekistan. In 1526, he led an army of 12,000 armored horsemen through the mountainous Khyber Pass from Afghanistan into the Punjab, won a great victory at Panjipat, and gave the Moguls a base in north India.

On Babur's death in 1530, Mogul rule stretched across almost the whole of northern India. Babur was succeeded by his son, Humayun (1508–1556), who inherited little of his father's political talent. The Moguls needed a more accomplished ruler, because they faced many challenges. Their own followers included many outsiders such as Afghans and Uzbeks with no loyalty to the dynasty. Afghan armies in eastern India allied with the independent ruler of Gujerat in the south to try to expel Mogul rule.

In 1539, Humayun suffered a defeat at the hands of the Afghans at the Battle of Chausa. He was driven into exile in Iran. In 1554, however, Humayun was able to reconquer northern India, recapturing Delhi the following year. After Humayun died, the crown passed to his son Akbar (1542–1605) (*see 3:408*).

Akbar and his successors established a lasting dynasty. Like their Mongol predecessors, the Moguls had few governmental structures and were heavily outnumbered by their Hindu subjects, so they based their rule on cooperation with local rulers and toleration of the Hindu religion. The Moguls established a luxurious court that emphasized their own status, which was also reflected in their monumental architecture . Eventually, they would bring more of India under the rule of one dynasty than at any time since the ancient empire of Ashoka in the third century B.C.E.

Babur's tomb stands in Kabul, Afghanistan, where his body was taken after his death. Babur's subjects claimed that he offered his life to God in order to save that of his son Humayun, who was gravely sick. Humayun recovered, and Babur went into a decline that ended within a year with his death.

Time Line

POLITICAL EVENTS IN EUROPE	CULTURAL EVENTS IN EUROPE	AFRICA AND ASIA

1200—

1209 Pope Innocent III recognizes the Franciscan order of friars

1206 Genghis Khan proclaims himself supreme leader of all Mongols. Muslim rule established over northern India.

1213 Genghis Khan invades China

1215 King John of England forced to sign the Magna Carta, giving rights and privileges to the nobles

1218 Genghis Khan invades central Asia

1223 First Mongol invasion of Russia

1226 Teutonic Knights begin to conquer Prussia and convert it to Christianity

1235 Mongols establish rule over northern China

1238 Mongols capture Moscow

1241 Commercial agreement between Lübeck and Hamburg marks beginning of future Hanseatic League

1243 Battle of Köse Dagh: Mongols reduce Seljuk Turks to vassal state

1250—

1255 Death of Sundiata, ruler of Mali

1260 Kublai Khan becomes Mongol leader

1266 Catholic scholar Thomas Aquinas begins his *Summa Theologiae*

1271 Marco Polo sets out on overland journey to China

1275 Marco Polo enters service of Kublai Khan

1279 Kublai Khan establishes rule over all of China and founds the Yuan dynasty

1281 Typhoon ends attempted Mongol invasion of Japan

1288 Turkoman amir Osman founds Ottoman dynasty

1295 Marco Polo returns to Venice

1297 Italian painter and architect Giotto paints frescoes in the Church of St. Francis in Assisi

1298 Marco Polo publishes his *Travels*

13th Century	14th Century	15th Century	16th Century	17th Century

POLITICAL EVENTS IN EUROPE	CULTURAL EVENTS IN EUROPE	AFRICA AND ASIA

1300—

1303 Pope Boniface VIII claims supreme political authority for the papacy; the French king imprisons him and he dies

c. 1314 Italian poet Dante Alighieri begins writing *The Divine Comedy*

1307 Accession of Mansa Musa ruler of Mali

1324 Mansa Musa makes pilgrimage to Mecca

1336 Kamakura shogunate in Japan overthrown; Ashikaga shogunate established

1337 Beginning of Hundred Years' War between England and France

1346 Battle of Crécy: English longbow proves effective against French cavalry

1348 Black Death (outbreak of bubonic plague) spreads across Europe. Foundation of University of Prague in Bohemia.

1350—

1354 Ottoman Turks establish military base at Gallipoli

1361 Ottoman Turks capture Adrianople

1364 Foundation of University of Cracow in Poland

1368 Ming dynasty established in China

1370 Teutonic Knights defeat Lithuanians at Rudau

1375 First European map of West Africa shows kingdom of Mali

1378 Beginning of the Great Schism: two rival popes claim authority over the Catholic Church

1378 English writer John Wycliffe attacks the role of pope and priests in the Catholic Church

1380 Mongols defeated by Dmitri Donskoi, prince of Moscow

1380 John Wycliffe publishes his translation of the Bible into English

1386 Poland and Lithuania united under the Jagiellon dynasty

c. 1387 English poet Geoffrey Chaucer begins writing *The Canterbury Tales*

1389 Battle of Kosovo: Ottoman Turks defeat the Serbians and their allies

1393 Tamerlane takes Baghdad

1397 Union of Colmar links Denmark, Norway, and Sweden

13th Century	14th Century	15th Century	16th Century	17th Century

132

POLITICAL EVENTS IN EUROPE	CULTURAL EVENTS IN EUROPE	AFRICA AND ASIA
	c. 1400 Beginnings of the Renaissance	1402 Battle of Ankara: Tamerlane defeats and captures Ottoman sultan Bayazid I 1405 Death of Tamerlane; his empire disintegrates
1400		
1410 1410 Battle of Tannenberg (Grünwald): Ladislaus II of Poland defeats Teutonic Knights	1415 Bohemian writer and preacher Jan Hus executed for heresy at Constance, Germany	
1417 End of the Great Schism: papacy reunified in Rome		
1419 Hussites, followers of Jan Hus, revolt against Holy Roman emperor		
1420	c. 1420 German mystic Thomas à Kempis writes *The Imitation of Christ*	
	c. 1426 Italian artist Tommaso Masaccio makes first attempts at perspective in painting	
1430		1433 The Great Withdrawal: Ming China ceases overseas exploration
1434 Cosimo de' Medici returns from exile to become ruler of Florence		
1440 1439 Ottoman Turks reconquer Serbia		
1450	c. 1450 Invention of Europe's first printing press	
1453 End of Hundred Years' War. Ottoman Turks capture Constantinople (Istanbul).		1453 Ottomans begin conversion of St. Sophia Basilica (Hagia Sophia) in Constantinople into a mosque
1454 Outbreak of Thirteen Years' War between Poland and the Teutonic Knights	1455 Gutenberg publishes the first printed edition of the Bible	

13th Century	14th Century	15th Century	16th Century	17th Century

POLITICAL EVENTS IN EUROPE	CULTURAL EVENTS IN EUROPE	AFRICA AND ASIA
1462 Accession of Ivan III as grand duke of Muscovy		**1461** Ottoman Turks capture Greek kingdom of Trebizond
1466 Peace of Thorn: Poland regains West Prussia and becomes feudal overlord of Teutonic Knights in East Prussia		**1463** Pope Pius II issues last call for a crusade against the Ottoman Turks
1469 Marriage of Ferdinand of Aragon and Isabella of Castile	**1470** Posthumous publication of the lyric poems of Petrarch (1304–1374)	**1468** Sunni Ali captures Timbuktu and founds the great African empire of Gao
1472 Ivan III, grand duke of Moscow, proclaims himself czar of Russia		
1476 Swiss defeat Charles the Bold, last duke of Burgundy		
1477 French defeat and kill Charles the Bold. Burgundian lands are divided between France and the Austrian Habsburgs.		
1478 Lorenzo de' Medici becomes sole ruler of Florence. Ivan III gains control of Novgorod.	**1479** Completion of Cathedral of the Assumption in the Kremlin, Moscow	
1480 Ivan III rejects Tatar overlordship		
1481 Ferdinand and Isabella attack Granada, the last Moorish kingdom in Spain		
1484 Ottoman Empire in Europe reaches Danube River		**1483** Shogun Ashikaga Yoshimasa builds the Silver Pagoda in Kyoto
1485 End of the Wars of the Roses in England	**1485** Posthumous publication of *De re Aedificatoria* by Italian architect Leon Batista Alberti (1404–1472)	
1486 Provence becomes part of France		**1487** The Chinese adopt a standard form of written exam for entry to the civil service
1492 Ferdinand and Isabella capture Granada		
	1494 Luca Pacioli, Italian developer of double-entry bookkeeping, publishes *Summa de Arithmetica*	
	1497 Leonardo da Vinci paints *The Last Supper*	
	1498 Italian monk Savonarola executed for heresy in Florence, Italy	

1460 — 1470 — 1480 — 1490 —

13th Century	14th Century	15th Century	16th Century	17th Century

POLITICAL EVENTS IN EUROPE	CULTURAL EVENTS IN EUROPE	AFRICA AND ASIA
	c. 1500 Beginning of inflation in Europe	
	1503 Michelangelo completes the sculpture *David*	
	c. 1504 Leonardo da Vinci paints the *Mona Lisa*	
	1506 Construction begins of St Peter's, Rome	
	1509 Erasmus publishes *The Praise of Folly*	
	1513 Italian philosopher Niccolò Machiavelli writes *The Prince*	**1514** Battle of Chaldiran: Ottoman Turks defeat Iranian army. European explorers arrive at Chinese court.
	1515 German theologian Johann Eck defends charging of interest on loans	
	1516 English humanist Thomas More publishes *Utopia*	**1516** Ottoman Turks defeat Egyptian Mamluks and conquer Syria and Arabia
	1517 German monk Martin Luther nails his Ninety-Five Theses to the door of Wittenberg Castle church to protest against practices of the Roman Catholic Church. The Protestant Reformation begins.	
	1521 Luther refuses to recant and receives backing from German princes	**1520** Accession of Ottoman emperor Süleyman
	c. 1522 Venetian artist Titian paints *Bacchus and Ariadne*	
1525 Peasants' revolt in Germany. They claim justification from Luther's teachings, but he rejects this.		
1526 Battle of Mohács, Hungary: Ottoman Turks defeat and kill Louis II of Hungary and Bohemia. Crown of Hungary and Bohemia passes to Habsburgs.		**1526** Turkish warrior Babur invades northern India and becomes first Mogul ruler
1529 Ottoman Turks besiege Vienna	**1528** Italian diplomat Count Baldassarre Castiglione publishes *The Courtier*	
1533 Marriage of Catherine de' Medici to Henry II of France	**1533** German painter Hans Holbein the Younger paints *The Ambassadors*	
1534 Henry VIII makes himself supreme head of the Church in England, in place of the pope		
1538 Last Venetian possessions in Aegean fall to Ottoman Turks		**1539** Mogul emperor Humayun, son of Babur, defeated by Afghans and driven into exile in Iran
	1545 Michelangelo completes tomb for Pope Julius II	
1547 Accession of Ivan IV of Russia (Ivan the Terrible)		

1500

1510

1520

1530

1540

13th Century	14th Century	15th Century	16th Century	17th Century

	POLITICAL EVENTS IN EUROPE	CULTURAL EVENTS IN EUROPE	AFRICA AND ASIA
1550	**1550** Ivan IV of Russia reforms local government to limit powers of nobles	**1550** Italian painter and architect Giorgio Vasari publishes *The Lives of the Artists*	
		1554 Italian composer Palestrina publishes his first book of masses	**1554** Humayun reconquers northern India
1560			**1556** Death of Humayun, accession of his son, Akbar
	1566 Beginning of Eighty Years' War: Dutch revolt against Spanish rule		
	1569 Poland and Lithuania form Commonwealth of the Two Nations		
1570	**1571** Battle of Lepanto: European coalition destroys Ottoman fleet, but Ottomans quickly regain control of eastern Mediterranean		**1571** Ottoman Turks conquer Tunis
1580	**1581** Ivan IV of Russia murders his son		
		1587 Italian composer Claudio Monteverdi composes his first book of madrigals	
		1589 Italian political theorist Giovanni Botero publishes *On the Reason of State*	
1600	**1598** Election of Boris Gudonov as czar of Russia		
		1607 Monteverdi writes opera *Orfeo*	
1610		**1609** First exchange bank opens in Amsterdam	
	1610 Polish army occupies Moscow; son of Polish king becomes czar		
	1612 Russians recapture Moscow. Michael Romanov elected czar, founding the Romanov dynasty.		
	1618 Protestant nobles in Bohemia revolt against Holy Roman emperor Ferdinand II, setting off the Thirty Years' War		**1618** Manchu establish kingdom in northeastern China
1630	**1630** Hanseatic League dissolved		
1640			**1637** Russian explorers in Siberia reach Pacific Ocean
		1642 Monteverdi writes opera *The Coronation of Poppea*	**1644** Manchu end Ming dynasty in China and establish their own Ching dynasty
1650			**1652** Dutch settlers arrive in southern Africa

13th Century	14th Century	15th Century	16th Century	17th Century

Glossary

absolutism a system of government in which the ruler has unrestricted power and is responsible to no one. Absolutism developed as the feudal system collapsed and monarchs grew in power.

alchemy a form of chemistry that originated in Alexandria about 100 B.C.E. and was still practiced in the Middle Ages. Alchemy aimed to find the elixir of life—a medicinal preparation that would prolong life—and a way of turning metals into gold.

astrolabe a navigational aid used for measuring the altitude of the sun or stars. It was widely used by mariners in the fifteenth and sixteenth centuries until superseded by the sextant.

bill of exchange a signed instruction to pay a sum of money to a specified person that emerged in the sixteenth century as a vital means of trade.

Black Death an epidemic of bubonic plague that killed up to 40 percent of the population of Europe between 1348 and 1377.

Byzantine Empire the Greek, Christian empire that ruled from Byzantium (Constantinople) from the fourth century. It survived until the Ottoman Turks captured Constantinople in 1453.

Calvinism a branch of Protestantism preached by followers of the French theologian John Calvin (1509–1564). Calvinism taught that people could achieve salvation only through God's grace not their own efforts and that God predestined history. Calvinism influenced Presbyterians, Puritans, and French Huguenots.

caravan a group of people and pack animals traveling together.

Christendom a term used in the late Middle Ages to refer to the Christian part of the world; it corresponded to the area we now call western Europe.

Confucianism a Chinese philosophy based on the teachings of Confucius (K'ung Fu-tse, c. 551–c.479 B.C.E.). It advocated an orderly life of public service and respect for tradition and authority.

crossbow a common weapon from the fourteenth century, comprising a horizontal bow fixed on a wooden stock. It was easier to use than a longbow and its short arrows, called bolts, could pierce armor.

crusades medieval military expeditions by European Christians to capture Palestine, or the Holy Land, from the Muslims.

Dominicans members of a Christian order of friars founded by St. Dominic of Spain in 1216. The order emphasized mental rather than physical labor, and Dominicans were important as teachers, preachers, and missionaries.

enclosure the process of fencing off fields and common land for private use. Sixteenth-century European landowners enclosed land in order to keep sheep. The process often deprived villagers of land they used to raise crops or graze animals.

feudal system a form of social organization, common in medieval Europe, that divided society into three estates: the nobility, the clergy, and everyone else. The estates were bound by a system of mutual duties and obligations. Lords provided protection for the peasants on their estates, for example; in return, peasants were tied to laboring in the service of the lord. The feudal system began to collapse in much of Europe in the early modern period.

Franciscans members of various Christian orders of friars based on the teachings of St. Francis of Assisi (c.1181–1226). The first Franciscan order was founded by St. Francis in 1209.

friar a member of certain Roman Catholic religious orders, including the Dominicans, Franciscans, Carmelites, and Augustinians. Unlike monks, friars preached and did missionary and social work. They often supported themselves by begging.

Genoese belonging to Genoa, an Italian city-state that was an important maritime power in the Mediterranean from about 1100 to 1400.

Golden Horde a part of the Mongol empire, established in 1241, and occupying what is now southern Russia and the Ukraine.

guild a medieval craft association formed to protect its members, maintain standards, and regulate the training of apprentices. From around the twelfth century, guilds grew to be very powerful in many European towns.

Hanseatic League a group of chiefly German cities that gained control of sea trade in the Baltic and North Sea in the fouteenth century but declined in the fifteenth.

heresy an opinion or belief that is contrary to the accepted doctrine, in particular of the Roman Catholic Church. In the fifteenth and sixteenth centuries, heresy was a serious crime and those found guilty of it were dealt with severely.

Hinduism a major world religion that is particularly important in India. Hinduism developed over several thousand years and worships many gods, including Brahma, Shiva, and Vishnu. Hindus believe in reincarnation.

Holy Roman Empire a central European empire of mainly Germanic states. The empire was ruled by an emperor elected by the most powerful German princes and had the pope as its spiritual head.

humanism a tradition of thought that emphasizes the needs and abilities of humankind. Modern humanism contrasted with medieval European ideas, which saw humanity as essentially sinful and earthly life as something to be despised.

icon a religious image, usually painted on wood, of God, Jesus, a saint, or the Virgin Mary. Icons form an important sacred tradition in Eastern Orthodox Christianity.

illuminated manuscripts medieval manuscripts containing bright-colored, painted ornamentation and decoration. Monks produced the earliest illuminated manuscripts, but from the 1200s on urban craftworkers took over their production.

inflation a general rise in prices in a country's economy, such that the same goods and services cost more than they did before.

Islam a major world religion, founded in the sixth and seventh centuries by the prophet Muhammad (c. 570–632). The followers of Islam, called Muslims, worship one god, Allah. Islam is split into two branches. Shia Islam is popular in Iran. Sunni Islam dominates the rest of the Islamic world.

Janissaries an elite military corps in the Ottoman Empire, recruited mainly from young Christians taken as tribute from their parents. Established in the 1300s, they were noted for their discipline but later became a threat to the sultan's authority and were outlawed in 1826.

Koran the holy book of Islam, containing the revelations of Allah to Muhammad.

kremlin a Russian word for "fortress." The kremlin in Moscow dates from the late fifteenth century and includes several cathedrals and palaces.

longbow a large bow that is held vertically and shoots a long arrow. It was the main weapon of English armies in the fourteenth and fifteenth centuries. It had great range but required skill and practice to use.

Lutheranism a major branch of Protestantism, based on the teachings of German theologian Martin Luther (1483–1546). Luther's protests against the Catholic Church triggered the Reformation. His chief doctrines concerned the authority of the Bible and salvation through faith, rather than through one's own moral efforts or good works.

Mamluks a group that emerged in the twelfth century as bodyguards to the sultans of Egypt. In 1250 they seized power. Rival Mamluk groups ruled Egypt until the Ottoman invasion in 1517 but retained great power until the nineteenth century.

monastery a building occupied by a community of monks who withdraw from the world to live according to rules of poverty and chastity, accompanied by regular praying and fasting.

Mongols a nomadic Asiatic people whose homeland is the area of modern Mongolia, to the north of China. In the thirteenth century, Genghis Khan united the Mongol tribes to conquer the largest land empire in history, stretching from far eastern Asia to eastern Europe.

Moors a name once given to Arabic-speaking Muslims of northwest Africa—modern Morocco, Algeria, Tunisia, and Mauretania. Moors and Arabs conquered Spain from 711 to 718 and created a Moorish kingdom noted for its architecture and culture.

Muslim a follower of Islam.

nation-state the main political entity of the post-medieval world, replacing the earlier feudal system. A nation state is a country with clearly defined borders, a central government more powerful than any local or regional authorities, and a population that gives primary allegiance to the nation rather than to anything inside or outside it.

New World a name given to the Americas by sixteenth-century Europeans.

Order of the Golden Fleece an order of knighthood established by Philip the Good, duke of Burgundy, in 1429. It was revived in 1713 by Charles VI of Austria for use in Austria and Spain.

Orthodox Christianity the main form of Christianity in Greece, Russia, and other parts of eastern Europe and western Asia. The Orthodox Church separated from Roman Catholicism because of longstanding differences in doctrine, especially concerning the authority of the pope.

Ottoman Empire a Muslim empire centered in Turkey that lasted from around 1300 to 1922. It was founded by the Ottoman Turks, nomads from central Asia.

parish a district with its own church and priest, in the Catholic church and some Protestant churches. In some countries, such as England, it also acts as the smallest unit of local government.

plague a fatal disease that appeared on numerous occasions in early modern Europe, killing great numbers of people. The disease, which was carried by fleas, caused fever, headache, sores, and enlarged glands in the groin and armpit. The Black Death, a particularly severe plague epidemic, killed between one-third and one-half of Europe's population in the fourteenth century.

Protestantism a major form of Christianity founded in western Europe in the sixteenth century, when many Christians separated from Catholicism.

reconquista the Spanish word for "reconquest". It is the name given to the campaign against the Moors of Granada begun in 1481 by the Spanish rulers Ferdinand and Isabella. Granada was the last surviving Islamic kingdom on the Iberian peninsula, and it was finally overthrown in 1492.

Reformation the religious movement in Europe in the sixteenth century that began as a reform movement within Roman Catholicism but led to the formation of separate Protestant churches.

Roman Catholicism a major world religion and the form of Christianity with the largest number of followers. The Roman Catholic Church, which is led by the pope from Rome, was western Europe's only form of Christianity until the Reformation of the early sixteenth century.

Rus a state centered in Kiev, in what is now Ukraine. It developed in the ninth century, when adventurers from Scandinavia known as Varangians set up trading bases on rivers between the Baltic and the Black Sea, and established their rule over the local Slavs. In 980 Kiev Rus was conquered by Vladimir I, ruler of the city of Novgorod. He converted to Christianity and made Rus a significant European power. In 1240 Mongol tribes conquered much of Rus. Northern areas later fell to Lithuania and Poland.

Safavid the Shia Muslim dynasty that ruled Iran from 1501 to 1722.

Schmalkaldic League a league of eight German princes and eleven German cities formed in 1531 for the purpose of defending the Lutheran faith. The league was a response to the decree made by the Diet of Augsburg in 1530 that all Lutherans should recognize the supremacy of the pope.

scholasticism the system of thought that dominated Christian theology in the later Middle Ages, reaching its peak in the 13th century. It was partly a response to new translations of the ancient Greek philosopher, Aristotle.

Shia a branch of Islam that is dominant in Iran. Shia separated from the Sunni majority over the question of the succession of political and religious authority following Muhammad's death in 632.

Slavs a group of peoples who spread through eastern and southeastern Europe between 200 and 600 C.E. In the tenth century, the Slavs split into three groups. The east Slavs became modern Russians, Byelorussians, and Ukrainians. The west Slavs became modern Poles, Czechs, and Slovaks. The south Slavs of the Balkan Peninsula became modern Croats, Serbs, Bulgarians, and Slovenes.

Spice Islands a group of islands in Indonesia, now called the Moluccas. They were famous from medieval times as the source of spices, such as cloves and nutmeg, that were highly valued in Europe.

Sunni the majority branch of Islam, numbering about 85 percent of all Muslims.

Teutonic Knights a group that developed in the twelfth century to organize German knights for the crusades. Later they set out to convert pagan areas of Europe to Christianity and conquered areas of what are now Poland, Lithuania, Latvia, and Estonia. They lost most of their power in the fourteenth century but controlled Latvia and Estonia for another 200 years.

tithes a donation or tax of a tenth on land or labor paid to a local church. In medieval times, tithes were the main source of income for Christian priests and their churches.

usury nowadays this means charging interest on loans of money at a very high rate, but in medieval Christian theology any charging of interest on loans of money was defined as usury, and, therefore, sinful.

vassal in the feudal system, a vassal was anyone who received something from a superior in return for service and loyalty. Peasants were vassals to their local lord, but lords were also vassals to greater lords, greater lords to their king, and even some kings to more powerful kings.

woodcut a picture or design printed from a block of wood (also the block itself). Sections of wood are cut away by the artist and what is left is coated with ink to produce the printed picture. Woodcuts began to be used as an artform in the 1400s. The woodcuts of Albrecht Dürer (1471–1528) are masterpieces of Western art.

Further Resources

Continuity and Change

Chambers, M., et al. *The Western Experience. Volume 1: To the Eighteenth Century*. New York: McGraw-Hill, 1995.

Detwiler, D. S. *Germany: A Short History*. Carbondale, IL: Southern Illinois University Press, 1976.

History of the Ancient and Medieval World, 12 vols. Tarrytown, NY: Marshall Cavendish Corporation, 1996.

Hollister, C. W. *Medieval Europe: A Short History*. New York: McGraw-Hill, 1998.

Jacobs, J., ed. *The Horizon Book of Great Cathedrals*. New York: American Heritage Publishing Co., 1968.

MacDonald, F. *The World in the Time of Leonardo Da Vinci*. Parsippany, NJ: Silver Burdett Press, 1998.

Palmer, R. R. and Colton, J. *A History of the Modern World to 1815*. New York: McGraw-Hill, 1995.

Pinkney, D. H. and De Sauvigny, G. B. *History of France*. Centreport, NY: The Forum Press, 1983.

Rice, E. F. and Grafton, A. *The Foundations of Early Modern Europe, 1460–1559*. New York: W. W. Norton & Co., 1994.

The World of Christendom

Collins, J. B. *The State in Early Modern France*. New York: Cambridge University Press, 1995.

Doran, S. *England and Europe in the Sixteenth Century*. New York: St. Martin's Press, 1999.

Eltis, D. *The Military Revolution of Sixteenth-Century Europe*. London: IB Tauris & Co., 1995.

Merrick, J. *Early Modern European History: Renaissance to 1789*. New York: Markus Wiener Publishing, 1988.

Smith, A. G. R. *The Emergence of a Nation State: The Commonwealth of England 1529–1660*. Reading, MA: Addison Wesley Publishing Company, 1997.

Strayer, J. R. *On the Medieval Origins of the Modern State*. Princeton, NJ: Princeton University Press, 1973.

Population and Agriculture

Gunst, P. *Agrarian Development and Social Change in Eastern Europe*. Brookfield, VT: Variorum, 1996.

Herlihy, D. *The Black Death and the Transformation of Europe*. Cambridge, MA: Harvard University Press, 1997

Platt, C. *King Death: The Black Death and its Aftermath in Late Medieval England*. Toronto, Ontario: University of Toronto Press, 1996.

Schmal, H. *Patterns of European Urbanisation Since 1500*. London: Routledge Kegan & Paul, 1981.

Sweeney, D., ed. *Agriculture in the Middle Ages: Technology, Practice, and Representation*. Philadelphia, PA: University of Pennsylvania Press, 1995.

Ziegler, P. *The Black Death*. New York: HarperCollins, 1971.

Trade and Wealth

Braudel, F. *Capitalism and Material Life 1400–1800*. Fontana 1974

——. *Civilization and Capitalism 15th–18th Century. Vol 1: The Structures of Everyday Life*. Berkeley, CA: University of California Press, 1992

——. *Civilization and Capitalism 15th–18th Century. Vol 2: The Wheels of Commerce*. Berkeley, CA: University of California Press, 1992.

——. *Civilization and Capitalism 15th–18th Century. Vol 3: The Perspective of the World*. Berkeley, CA: University of California Press, 1992.

Jardine, L. *Worldly Goods: A New History of the Renaissance*. London: Papermac, 1996.

Kamen, H. *European Society 1500–1700*. New York: Unwin Hyman, 1984.

Scholasticism and the Universities

Giuberti, F. *Materials for a Study on Twelfth Century Scholasticism*. Amherst, NY: Prometheus Books, 1982.

Langholm, O. I. *The Legacy of Scholasticism in Economic Thought: Antecedents of Choice and Power*. New York: Cambridge University Press, 1998.

Pedersen, O. *The First Universities: Studium Generale and the Origins of University Education in Europe*. New York: Cambridge University Press, 1998.

Plott, J. *Global History of Philosophy: The Period of Scholasticism*. South Asia Books, 1990.

Southern, R. W. *Scholastic Humanism and the Unification of Europe: Foundations*. Malden, MA: Blackwell Publishing, 1995.

Humanism and the Spread of Knowledge

Cassirer, E., ed. *Renaissance Philosophy of Man*. Chicago, IL: University of Chicago Press, 1956.

Demolen, R., ed. *Erasmus of Rotterdam: A Quincentennial Symposium*. New York: Irvington Publishing, 1971.

Gilmore, M. P. *The World of Humanism, 1453–1517*. Westport, CT: Greenwood Publishing Group, 1983.

Hale, J. *Machiavelli and Renaissance Italy*. New York: Macmillan Inc., 1960.

Kristeller, P. O. *Renaissance Thought and the Arts: Collected Essays*. Princeton, NJ: Princeton University Press, 1990.

Olin, J., ed. *Christian Humanism and the Reformation: Selected Writings of Erasmus*. New York: Fordham University Press, 1987.

Social Structures

Black, M. *Feudal Society: Social Classes and Political Organization*. Chicago, IL: University of Chicago Press, 1982.

Duby, G. *The Knight, The Lady, and the Priest: The Making of Modern Marriage in Medieval France.* Chicago, IL: University of Chicago Press, 1994.

Gies, F. *Marriage and the Family in the Middle Ages.* New York: HarperCollins, 1989.

Stone, L. *Family, Sex and Marriage in England 1500–1800.* New York: HarperCollins, 1986.

Van Os, H. *The Art of Devotion in the Late Middle Ages in Europe.* Princeton, NJ: Princeton University Press, 1995.

Vauchez, A. *The Laity in the Middle Ages: Religious Beliefs and Devotional Practices.* Notre Dame, IN: University of Notre Dame Press, 1997.

The Renaissance and the Arts

Burckhardt, J. *The Civilization of the Renaissance in Italy.* New York: Penguin U.S.A., 1990.

Kerrigan, W. and Brach, G. *The Idea of the Renaissance.* Baltimore MD: John Hopkins University Press, 1991.

Hartt, F., ed. *History of Italian Renaissance Art,* 4th edn. New York: Harry N. Abrams Publishing, 1994.

Murray, L. L. *The High Renaissance and Mannerism: Italy, the North, and Spain 1500–1600.* New York: Thames and Hudson, 1985.

Murray, P. *The Architecture of the Italian Renaissance.* New York: Schocken Books, 1997.

Murray, P. and Murray, L.L. *Art of the Renaissance.* New York: Thames and Hudson, 1985.

Pope-Hennessy, J. *Italian Renaissance Sculpture, Vol 1.* New York: Random House, 1986.

The Margins of Europe

Crummey, R. O. *The Formation of Muscovy, 1304–1613.* Reading, MA: Addison Wesley Publishing Company, 1987.

Davis, N. *Heart of Europe: A Short History of Poland.* New York: Oxford University Press, 1986.

Dmytryshyn, B., ed. *Medieval Russia: A Source Book, 850–1700.* Austin, TX: Holt Rinehart & Winston, 1997.

Martin, J. *Medieval Russia, 980–1584.* New York: Cambridge University Press, 1996.

Rowell, S. C. *Lithuania Ascending: A Pagan Empire Within East-Central Europe, 1295–1345.* New York: Cambridge University Press, 1994.

The Ottoman Turks

Goodwin, J. *Lords of the Horizon: A History of the Ottoman Empire.* New York: Henry Holt & Co., 1999.

Inalck, H., ed. *An Economic and Social History of the Ottoman Empire, 1300–1914.* New York: Cambridge University Press, 1995.

Itzkowitz, N. *Ottoman Empire and Islamic Tradition.* Chicago, IL: University of Chicago Press, 1980.

Lord Kinross. *Ottoman Centuries: The Rise and Fall of the Turkish Empire.* New York: William Morrow & Co., 1988.

Lewis, B. *Istanbul and the Civilization of the Ottoman Empire.* Norman, OK: University of Oklahoma Press, 1989.

Kafador, C. *Between Two Worlds: The Construction of the Ottoman State.* Berkeley, CA: University of California Press, 1995.

Woodhead, C., ed. *Süleyman the Magnificent and His Age: The Ottoman Empire in the Early Modern World.* Reading, MA: Addison Wesley Publishing Company, 1995.

Developments in Africa

Diamond, J. *Guns, Germs, and Steel: The Fates of Human Societies.* New York: W. W. Norton & Co., 1998.

Diop, C. A. *Precolonial Black Africa: A Comparative Study of the Political and Social Systems of Europe and Black Africa.* Lawrenceville, NJ: Red Sea Press, 1990.

Isichei, E. *Africa Before 1800.* London: Longman Group UK, 1984.

Kostow, P. and King, M. L., Jr. *Centuries of Greatness: The West African Kingdoms 750–1900.* Broomall, PA: Chelsea House Publishing, 1995.

Niame, D. T., ed. *Africa from the Twelfth to the Sixteenth Century.* Berkeley, CA: University of California Press, 1986.

Vogel, J. and Vogel, J. O. *Encyclopaedia of Precolonial Africa: Archaeology, History, Languages, Cultures and Environments.* London: Altamira Press, 1997.

Developments in Asia

Hansen, V. *Changing Gods in Medieval China.* Princeton, NJ: Princeton University Press, 1990.

Hymes, R. P., ed. *Ordering the World: Approaches to State and Society in Sung Dynasty China.* Berkeley, CA: University of California Press, 1993.

Martell, H. *Imperial China 221 B.C. to A.D. 1294.* Austin, TX: Raintree/Steck Vaughn, 1998.

Shiba, Y. *Commerce and Society in Sung China.* Ann Arbor, Michigan: Centre for Chinese Studies, 1970.

Illustration Credits

Index

Aachen *21*, 50
Abelard, Peter 51
accounting system, of Pacioli 45, 48
Adrianople 100
Africa, empires 109–118
Aka people 116–117
Akbar, Mogul emperor 130
Akuta 122
Alberti, Leon Battista *80*
Albrecht, duke of Bavaria 85
Alcázar *24*
alchemy 56
Alexander, grand duke of Lithuania 93
Alexander VI, Pope 11
Algeria *111*
Almagest (Ptolemy) 53
Almoravids 112, 115
Ambassadors, The (H. Holbein the Younger) *88*
Amsterdam 44, 48
Anabaptists 17
Anatolia 101
Ankara 101
Annam 127
Antwerp 40, 42, 44–45
Aquinas, Thomas 57, *58*
Aquitaine *13*
Aragon 23–24
Archimedes 52
architecture, Renaissance 88
Aristotle 57, 64, 73
armor 15
army/armies, European 26–27, 72–73, 76
arquebus 26, *27*
artillery 26
Ascensius, Iodocus *66*
Ashikaga shogunate 127
Asia, and Europe *41*, 119–120
astrology 56
Augustine of Hippo 56–57
Auvillar, market hall *40*
Averroës (Ibn Rushd) *57*
Avignon, antipope established at 20

Babur, Mogul emperor *129*, 130
Bacchus and Ariadne (Titian) *84*
banks 44, 48
    Fugger banking dynasty 46–47
Bantu 111, 116–117
Bartolommeo, Fra, painting by *58*
Basil IV Shuisky, czar of Russia 97
Battle Between Carnival and Lent, The (Breughel the Elder) *11*
Bayezid I, sultan of the Ottoman empire 101
Beauvais, cathedral roof 7, *18*
Beijing 119, 123, 128–129
Bellini, Gentile *104*
Benin *112*, 113
Berber people 110, 112
Bergen *16*
Bernard of Clairvaux 11
Beynac Castle *13*
Bible 60, *61, 62*
bills of exchange 48
Bithynia 99
Black Death 8–9, 30, *31,* 43–44, 93
Black Sea *108*

Bodleian Library (Oxford) *53*
Bohemia 93, 94, 95
Bokhara 123
Bologna, university 50, 51, *52, 56*
Book of Hours, French *35*
bookbinding *33*
bookkeeping 45
books 56–57, 60–62, 66, 80
Borgia, Cesare *85*
Bosch, Hieronymus *34*
Bosworth Field, Battle of (1485) 23
Botero, Giovanni 70
Botticelli, Sandro, painting by *87*
boyars 96, 97, 98
Bramante, Donato 84
Brethren of the Common Life 54
Breughel the Elder, Pieter *11*
Brittany 23
Brunelleschi, Filippo *79, 81*
Brussels 16
Buddhism *125, 126,* 127
Bulgaria, and the Ottomans 101
Burgundy 23, 25–28
Buridan, Jean 56
Byzantine empire 64, 92
    Orthodox Christianity 10
    and the Ottomans 16–18, 19, 100–101, 103

cabala 66
Calais 23
Calvin, John 10
Calvinism 95
Cambridge, university 52, *53*
Cameroon, Bantu language 117
Canterbury Tales, The (Chaucer) 50
Capet, Hugh, king of France 12
Casimir IV, king of Poland 91–93
Castagno, Andrea del, painting by *63*
Castiglione, Baldassare 9
Castile 23, 24, 71–72
Cathay 119
cathedrals 65
    schools 54
Catholic Church
    and education 52, 56–57, 78
    Great Schism 11, 20
    and humanism 68
    pre-Reformation 10–11
    reform *17*
    sale of indulgences 11–12, 46
    and universities 52, 58
    and usury 44, 73
cereals 33
Chaldiran, Battle of (1514) 105
Champagne, fairs 40
Chao Kou 122
Charlemagne 12, 20, *21, 50*
Charles V, Holy Roman emperor, and the Schmalkaldic League 47
Charles the Bold, duke of Burgundy 25, 26
Chartres, cathedral 7
Chaucer, Geoffrey 50
Chausa, Battle of (1539) 130
China
    Confucianism 18, 40, 66
    encyclopedia (11,000 volumes) 66
    Great Withdrawal 127–128
    gunpowder 66, 121
    Manchu (Ching) dynasty 128–129
    Ming dynasty 16, 18, *120,* 127–128
    Sung dynasty 120–123
    trade 18, 113
    Yuan dynasty 123–125, 127
Chokwe people *116*
Christendom, decline 20–21, 68

churches, and humanism *64,* 65
Cicero 63
cities and towns 16, 36, 77
    fortifications 73
    shops *73,* 77, *78*
    See also urbanization
class/rank, social 75–76
    and the feudal system 8, 13–14
clergy, educated 49, 50, 78
Cluny 11
coins 42, 45, *73*
Colleoni, Bartolomeo *82*
Colmar, Union of 24
Cologne *37*
Columbus, Christopher 24, 65
common law 72
condottiere 26
Confucianism 18, 40, 66, 124, 127–128
Confucius 124
conquistadores 18
Constance, Council of (1415) 94
Constantine XI Palaeologus Dragases 102
Constantinople, capture by Ottomans 16–18, 19, 26, 41, 52, 92, 99, 102, *103,* 104
copper, African 114
Coronation of Poppea, The (Monteverdi) 84
corregidors 71–72
Cosimo I (Cosimo de' Medici) 83, 87
Courtier, The (B. Castiglione) 9
Cracow, university 94
Crècy, Battle of (1346) 15
Cromwell, Thomas 30–31
crossbows 15, 26
Crusades 16, 90, *101,* 102
currency, paper 121
Cusa, Nicholas de 79–80
customs barriers 42
Cyprus, and the Ottomans 108
czars 96

Dante Alighieri 50
Danzig 16, 93
Dark Ages 53
Delhi 130
demesnes 34
Denmark, and the Union of Colmar 24
devshirme 102, 104
Diamond, Jared 116
Divine Comedy, The (Dante) 50
Dmitry, False 97
Dominicans 11, 50
Dürer, Albrecht 42, *46,* 88

Eastern Orthodox Church 10, 90
    Russian Orthodox Church 92
Eck, Johann 44
Edirne 100, *107*
education
    and the rise of humanism 59–68, 80
    the spread of learning in Europe 49–58, 59–62, 78
Egypt, Mamluks 105–107
Eighty Years' War (1568–1648) 44
Elbe River 42
Elizabeth of York *23*
enclosure 34–35, 36
encyclopedias, Chinese 66
England
    common law 72
    enclosures 34–35
    growth of a centralized monarchy 23
    Hundred Years' War (1338–1453) 8, *13, 14*–15

141

Page numbers in *italic type* refer to illustrations and captions.

Page numbers in *italic type* refer to illustrations and captions.

Page numbers in *italic type* refer to illustrations and captions.

Page numbers in *italic type* refer to illustrations and captions.